CLIMBING UP FROM THE DEPTHS

POEMS BY LOREN DENNY

LOREN DENNY

Order this book online at www.trafford.com
or email orders@trafford.com

Most Trafford titles are also available at major online book retailers.

Printed in the United States of America.

ISBN: 978-1-4907-5086-6 (sc)
ISBN: 978-1-4907-5088-0 (hc)
ISBN: 978-1-4907-5087-3 (e)

Library of Congress Control Number: 2014919994

Trafford rev. 02/11/2015

www.trafford.com

North America & international
toll-free: 1 888 232 4444 (USA & Canada)
fax: 812 355 4082

Acknowledgement

For Mom, Pops, and 'Ma' James: Thank you for the support and love you have given me, especially during my years of addiction and rehabilitation. Without you, there would be no book.

L.D.

My Balloons

You're my big red balloon
    bright-colored with size
You'll be tied to my arm soon
    as I watch with anxious eyes
My big red balloon
    once I had one of yellow
Bit by my brother
    silly little fellow
My big red balloon
    there's a blue one I miss
Popped on the ceiling
    careless, I guess
My big red balloon
    I hope our time's right
Unlike my pink one
    last seen in flight
My big red balloon
    now tied to my arm
You'll be mine forever
    if I keep you from harm

Dedicated to Jordan, Autumnlynn, and Matthew – Love you kids!!

Contents

ADDICTION

CLIMBING UP FROM THE DEPTHS

LOVE

INTROSPECTION

REFLECTIONS

ADDICTION

Descent

All angels are priceless and none has ever been born in Hell
I have walked with burnt wings and been many bad places, can't
    you tell?

Flames of the devil's breath scorched my soul, that's the smell
With my helpless cries, pitched so shriekingly loud, my soul
    shattered and fell

My lifeless descent so far downward now, no one can hear my yell
Fractured pieces of a broken angel without wings, up for auction,
    for sale

Ogre

I grind your bones to dust just to make my bread
I hurt everyone around me with things I've done and said
I had better change my ways of life and thinking, my head of lead
Unless I want to be alone forever and almost left for dead

Addiction my paradigm as I mold myself from one moment to the
next
Conundrums of introspect crippling life by being taken way out of
context
Quality living and solutions for unlike minds are never that
complex
Joy, love, and peace suffer, ever sober, from addiction's lingering
effects

Hunted

Have I, the hunter, become my own prey?
Followed my own scent trail for years, to kill me someday

All this time in life did I bait all the traps and snares?
To just find out that with my killing of me, no one cares

If so, now how do I go back and cover my tracks?
As now, I am scared to get hit by my stalker's next attack

I must be aware, vigilant, and on the defense
My, how this dilemma I'm in has gotten intense

Now I feel short of breath, tired, as if on borrowed, hunted time
Who will be the victor? The pressing shadowy hunter or the
    shadowy, addicted prey in mind?

Vanishing Cream

Three wishes I would wish for upon the now

First is to leave this relentlessly unforgiving, forsaken town
To grab my best friends and hit the dusty trail
As anything's better than how I have trapped myself in this
personal hell

Second is to find the intestinal fortitude to carry on
To find my happiness and peace spiritually within the parameters
of right, not wrong

Lastly, I would wish for clarity and retrospective of my life and
time and the things I've seen
Just to wipe it all away with vanishing cream

Mud

The feeling of being stuck in the mud, worn out, tired from
    running the race
Plain as day for all to see, evidenced by the scars all over his face

He once had some dreams of one day doing some traveling,
    starting a family, and settling down
But he and time got lost and things got so crazy with his pain and
    his disease, he got too scared to get around

As that dream died, so did others, like having a peaceful soul or
    being respected by his next of kin
Came and went was the dream of a life of honor, dignity, and
    spiritual service less life's sins

Gone in living were his dreams, carried by a sick and lonely
    existence of an uncompromising painful ghost
Dreams, with him and his disease, laid to rest at an early age, not
    noticed by family or most

Ill

Some kill
Let's deal
Others steal
Concrete, steel

Self will
Blood spill
Life skill
Cold chill

Ill will
Can't feel
Climbed hill
Criminal mill
No bills
Heart still

Layers peel
Revolving wheel
Can't heal

No thrill
Brain drill
Big pill
Window sill

Last meal
For real

Empty till
Chances nil

Psycho Mio

I am waiting this dawn to say I'm really sorry
Often the blood in my heart so black and tarry
Like a seine through the ocean that sweeps me away
When I crawl out of the netting, I make light of the fray
Like a bug on a limb, I'm brought down by my antics
All seems so well until eaten by the mantis
At times in a fog, walking around in hypnosis
Maybe I really do suffer from this psychosis
For as certain as I write this while sitting in jail
All the signs are there now, it's just me who can't tell

Stuff

My mind's in overdrive
Take the darkest ride
Cannot stand to lie
Scars I won't ever hide

Feelings of regret
Life's my biggest debt
Table has been set
Swear there's nothing left

People that I grift
Pain I cannot lift
Dangers that I kissed
Functions I have missed

Did it now and then
Not sure where I've been
It's my recurring sin
Patience wearing thin

Fitting in, getting tough
Crowded gatherings are rough
God, I hate this stuff
I cannot get enough

Pirate's Dream

A pirate's dream
The entrapped screams
My shoulder leans
The shattered dreams

God's forsaken
Chances taken
Camaraderie fakin'
Money makin'

Crashing heights
Try to fight
Shameless nights
Loss of rights

Weak, not strong
Right from wrong
Same ol' song

Something's not right
Chest so tight
A dangerous plight
Second sight

Where's the cabbage
Carry my baggage
All bad habits
Look at the damage

To none confessed
Nothing is blessed
Smoking the best
Laid some to rest

The ultimate fate
Life of hate
Before the magistrate
Death the freight

Acts of deception
Not using contraception
No tracks of affliction
All acts of addiction

Product to tout about
Too scared to walk about
Family member not talked about

A life less the fun
Nowhere to run
No chance for sun
Days, months, years, done

Misery

Summer Rain; How the clouds' darkness eases all my pain
The Smell; Refreshes the stench of my rotting soul
Washes Away; Some of my life's living stain
Brings Hope; That one day soon I will see my last rainbow

Summer Days; nothing can ever bring me down faster
Places Been; I have tortured myself town to town
Lord; Take my life and prove now You are the master
Never; Give me another reason to smile – I prefer a frown

Show Me; Cloudy days that signify the black of my heart
Put away; The sun forever, just for me
One More; Sun-filled day and I may make my afterlife start
Give; Me death to end my current misery

Devil's Loom

The whimsical mist of a choking fog
A punctured organ by a rabid dog

Tied to the revolving door, fear, no way to get through
Kaleidoscopic visions, I can't really be you

Game worthy beasts prevail, to embrace death is to win
Skipping stones across pools of blood, count me in

Vaults of dashed goals fill halls that lead to Satan's rooms
Devoid of hope in the spiritless fabric, the tawdry weave, of the
    Devil's loom

Cynicism

As surely as the sun shall rise and today my feet when I walk hit
the ground
My disease says "prepare for total darkness", lying to me without a
word or sound

I hear it say "all will be just fine", then it screams "touch me!"
when I'm at my lowest
"Can't you tell I am your only friend in the world as evidenced by
the 'did show' and 'did not show' list?"

"Old friend," it says, "you can let me in, just trust in you. You
know you can manage"
"Just open the door for me and when I am asked, I will leave
without all the damage"

"Won't you look at how your life and strength have grown?
Together, we won't go back"
"I am not the evil that they say. I'm not the problem I was then,
poised for my next attack'

"Don't you love the stars and how you shine with your voice so
strong, so lyrical?"
"Won't you bridge the gap inside you, now that you need me
most? Don't be cynical"

"I've heard about your hurdles and trials that you're having
difficulty getting over"
"Together, we can change the world and what really matters,
instead of climbing over every thought of going under"

"Confide in me and gain the strength to conquer all beyond the
walls of your own house"
"From our beginning together, it was all of them who lied to you,
not I, who made the man into a mouse"

Days Into Weeks

Devilish grin
Out again

Sins begin
Getting thin

White hype
Light pipe

Creep around
Without a sound

Paranoid
New toys

Take call
Drop ball

Vegas trips
Quag rips

Take run
Make some

Always late
Doomed fate

Sex freaks
Mind tweeks

Days into weeks

Reality's Desire

Sure seems now that life is quickly changing
My mind's impulse control is misbehaving

I can't seem to stop my actions or their bleeding
Nor the abundant growth in the Devil's fields I've been
    overseeding

I need to take a good look in the mirror and take a quick step back
Before I launch on me the pain of my next personal attack

I have had feelings like these so many times before today
Desperation and gloom and addiction I continually put in living
    my life's way

Surfacing now are blanketed emotions from a time I had hoped
    I'd forgot
Bubbling up now that I am sober, thought after concerning
    thought
My reality is my demise, leaving me empty now and emotionally
    distraught

I Got Game

I get my game on
Put the sting on
Work my next con
Then get long gone

Town is gettin' gritty
Money by committee
Ride to the nearest city
Nothing less than 250

What's that awful funk?
Tell you it's a skunk
Put him in the trunk
He just ran out of luck

Battery out the phone
Gotta' go it all alone
Do when as in Rome
Tell them I'm not home

'bout to make a stop
God, I hate the cops
Just a bunch of lops
I'm a-come out on top

How much in the package?
Don't let no one help bag it
Got no sleep but got to manage
It's my way of makin' cabbage

Tomorrow do it all again
Trust no family or friends
Go to church now and again
Pretend I'm free of sin

Think I'm being followed
Cars I have to borrow
My only plan for tomorrow
Keep my Mom from sorrow

Judas Brew

Why can't I change or just become you?
Because the Devil's work is all I do

The few times I'm slowed enough to open my eyes
I realize my life has no reason or rhyme
It becomes clear with no great surprise
That living in my body is just like doing time

I feel so small, this menial existence of mine
As if I am perpetually in life's cauldron, becoming food for the
    thoughtless
Being mixed in as part of the Judas brew
Serving myself up on a plate for the godless

There is no end in sight, even with damning recourse
For all who got caught in my wake, I am sorry!
I have lived a regretful life of terrible remorse

Why can't I change or just become you?
Because I'm food for the Devil, Satan's stew

Alcohol

Alcohol
10 feet tall

Life is great
Man I'm late

Glad to see ya
Margarita

Ho hum
Gin and Rum

7 and 7
Poured from heaven

Whiskey sour
Happy hour

Double up
Drugged up

Enhanced sex
Life perplexed

I'll drive
D.U.I

What went wrong
Head on

Hit the curb
Words I slurred

Got no thesis
Life in pieces

I'm fine
Doin' time

Sadness filled
Who'd I kill?

Let out
Turn about

Sobered up
Where's my cup

Stop too late
Death's the fate

Schizoid

Troubled boy

Diagnosed schizoid

Life destroyed

Doc's annoyed

Peer devoid

Evil deployed

One to avoid

Trust void

Pill toyed

Paranoid

Man droid

Living hemorrhoid

Cover tabloid

Ever unemployed

Love unenjoyed

Me

Me
I've always been all about me
Along my way, I've lost my grasp and my key to unlock the hasp
My face has finally run out of masks
    Me
I've always been all about me
And I have always been my biggest fear
I proved that when I landed in here
Traded all my freedom for perpetual tears

Me
I've always been all about me
Center of my own world, stuck on myself
I put everyone and everything on a shelf
Now it's no surprise no one will help

Me
I've always been all about me
As I now scream so loudly from inside
Cursing feeling, smitten due to rules I don't abide
A constant chance my life on the wrong side

Me
I've always been all about me
Your feelings have never mattered
In faith your trust I will shatter
Peace or addiction, I prefer the latter

Me
I've always been all about me
No need to read between the lines
I'm a 30-year addict still doin' time
I've always lied and said I'm fine
All the while I've been out of my mind

Schizocontrarian

My life at times is so erratic
With joy-filled tears and smiles of sadness
It seems as though it's really not mine
An empty brain in a body always bracing for impact while clothed
    with insanity
A tortuous feeling bringing so much pleasure
Life's grip always slipping through my clenched fingers
Sustaining little foundation, asking loved ones for forgiveness
Often being judged by visionaries who are so blinded
Tossed around on calm seas without tranquil shores in sight nor
    an island to walk to
So I ask you now, calmly, as I scream, stepping forward into the past
Are you truly my friend, or are you poised for attack?

I Can

Just in case I should forget where I am
I can listen for a few minutes and hear distant guard's keys in hand

I can remove my shoes and feel cold cement under my socks
I can try to use my comb with missing teeth to comb my locks

I can walk forty-five feet and visit ninety people in their dwellings
I can close my eyes at night and still see the terror of others yelling

I can differentiate and separate the food, yet not any of its flavor
I can feel a resentment of sorts in a life filled with anger

I can tell you we are a segregated bunch with only men around men
I can tell you my number and it's mine, but not to a cell phone
I can tell you it's one that I earned and I did it to me all alone

I can see you twice a week, and beyond an hour our time has passed
I can feel regret and pain as I can only touch you through Plexiglas

I can tell you a lie that I don't belong in this kingdom
I can also tell you the truth now – I played Russian roulette with
   my freedom

Hope Is a Kaleidoscope

An unimaginable day
Inability to fly away

Unblossoming progression
Encompasses depression

A challenging gauntlet
Blasphemy rampant

No cordial demeanor
Children unseen here

Unconditionally wicked
Traumatically twisted

Distastefully cunning
Extensively stunning

Spiritually forsaken
Emotionally taken

Criminal credentials
Ancestors influential

Empathetic inabilities
Problematic totalities

Hope's kaleidoscopic prism
Catastrophically imprisoned

Addiction sustained
Institutionally insane

Too Late

I am the bait
I miss my mate
The game I hate
Up too late
Sealed my fate
A panic state
My eyes dilate
Work. Pyrex plate
Teach and demonstrate
Led to magistrate
No release date
A lawyer mediates
Reason to hate
Parallels don't deviate
Meth I make
Quit too late

Retrospect

In receiving this time in which I sit and reflect
And take a good look at me, now and then, in retrospect

Taking this opportunity to judge me without malice or bias
To seek out the truth less those who lie to us

I'll take this time now while I'm in this state of mind
To become a better person, maybe a bit less selfish, less to do about
    what's yours and what's mine

Am I here behind these walls, these bars, because I've run aground
    spiritually?
Or is it because I'm missing a calling of sorts of whom I'm
    supposed to be?

Knowing quite well the colors of life diminish with each passing
    day, this much is true
At what point will I allow me to live free without the black and blue?

So if I am given a new day tomorrow by my Lord, by my Savior
Will I be able to change the burnt taste on the tongue of my life
    without flavor?

Reverse Enamor

Troubles begin
Fix is in
No, not again
Cold and thin

Addictions fight
Hide from sight
Downward flight
Nothing right
My chest so tight

Living is the cost
Issues flossed
Morality tossed
Love lost
Getting sauced

Reverse enamor
No glamour
Speech stammer
Jails clamor
Life's hammer

Color Me

Color me, in any weather, day or night
Color me and guide me, Lord, with your light

Color me with all your comfort and love
Color me, fill my sky with your beautiful doves

Color me divine up and down, east to west
Color me, give to my soul unwaivered peace

Color me, even if only for a short while
Color me, afford me a single reason to smile

Color me so my inspirations are free to roam
Color me, make me feel not so alone

Color me, show me how to change so it's not so hard
Color me, cover up my internal and external scars

Color me, dry my eyes and river of tears
Color me, make me safe and take away my fears

Color me with wonderful sights and amazing smells
Color me, pull me out of this living hell

Color me, so I may feel my heart again
Color me, take away all the damage from my sins

Color me, 'cause it's been so very tough
Color me, show me there's a better way
Color me, I may take my life today

Cranium

I have so damn many phobias

One of which is the country Syria

Another as a fact is Libya

Bite my nails off in mania

Do you feel that I am afraid of ya?

Cannot look into the eyes of ya

Inner screams of mass hysteria

White coats coming to take me away from ya

My words not right, it is dyslexia

Flowers on my casket, wisteria

Problem was inside my cranium

Hi

Well hello, my good friend, tell me, where have you been?
I've been infecting this world, sisters, brothers, and next of kin

But you have been gone for so long, why embrace you again?
Because I am the keeper of time and the director of sin

Well I am so glad to see you, so won't you come in?
Do you mind if I stay a while and turn the now into then?

You know you've always been welcome here since way back when
Knowing all the while your business here is to make mice of men

Fray

Maybe I am just a fool for having a dream
Like a love that soars as high as Earth's jet stream
To jump into the limelight as a bright beam
In becoming part of a family's fabric without being the seam

Find a happiness that in life leads my way
Gathers strength each and every day
Comforts me and others in knowing exactly what to say
Be trusted, with a life of joy and peace, away from the fray

Like Me

If you're like me, then you can hear the angels singing
If you're like me, then you're touching the doorbell to the Pearly
    Gates, it's ringing

If you're like me, then you feel your time on earth is ending soon
If you're like me, your soul is shaking. In death is where your
    living sins loom

If you're like me, you thought there would be time left for forgiveness
If you're like me, you were sure at some point you could shake off
    your sickness

If you're like me, your life was full speed ahead and "come 'n get
    ya some"
If you're like me, then you realize it was a lifestyle you should have
    quickly run from

If you're like me, you look at your relationships with your God,
    family, and friends with a great sadness
If you're like me, when it's all over, you feel you will meet it alone
    and with overall gladness

30 Years

30 years now the addict and starting over in my sobriety

30 years now of my not giving the world who I am supposed to be

30 years now, throughout the time period, only glimpses of hope

30 years now without forgiveness, spirituality, direction, no peace,
no hope

30 years now of others saying "Boy, what you could have been"

30 years now the weight on my chest, retrospect, and where do I
now begin

30 years now avoiding the questions, the who, why, what, all so
wrapped in fear

30 years now, I now realize, in jail, that I am a lucky man just to
be here

My Oh My

Times forgot
Guidelines not taught
Dreams I lost
Fears I fought

Sinking suspicions
Unfounded fruition
Praying position
No one who listens

Broken inside
Horrible ride
Ready to die
My oh my

Circus clown
'round and 'round
New way down
No sacred ground

Eye to eye
Why try?
Wonder why
I'd rather die?

Broken home
No dial tone
All alone
Skin and bone

Addict unadjusted
None trusted
Getting busted
Death thrusted

Shake the fall
Make the call
Stand tall
Not alone after all

Hide My Head

Hide my head
Or it's me you see

Hide my head
Control the fear in me

Hide my head
The shame is real

Hide my head
It's me I kill

Hide my head
Alone in the dark

Hide my head
My life's left no mark

Hide my head
For what I've done

Hide my head
I'm simply no one

Hide my head
From the pain inside

Hide my head
Nowhere to hide

Hide my head
Thirty years, still an addict

Raise my head
No longer have to have it

Half Day

So I have some work to do
Looking back at my life, it's nothing new

Focus on my issues to open up my filthy cage
Stop this act on stage and separate myself from the rage

End the addict behaviors, a mindset of entitlement, and "got to
  have its"
Take a good, honest look at my faults, that is if I can stand it

Now is the time for me to celebrate life without the drinking and
  drugs
I am not concerned if you don't believe me. I see your shoulder shrugs

When I made it sober through this morning into what some
  consider midday
Then I realized I met another goal, not to drink or drug through
  half my day

With that accomplished, I set a new goal, with it I pray
God, give me the strength just not to use for the rest of today

Drive

As I get older, I think about what it will take to change this man
When I've been so set in my ways for so long, it's hard to
    understand

My life's highways always seem to end up on a dead-end street
Each time I travel down it, I crash, same old song played, same beat

Tomorrow is another chance for me to change, even if just a little
But each day that tomorrow brings, I drive on and play the same
    old fiddle

Hope one day soon I can kiss my life's painful songs goodbye
The thought of losing my hurt someday brings tears to my eyes

Four-leaf Clover

Surely I couldn't have imagined using my disease, addiction, for
    others, to help them
By going to speak at meetings or high schools, having them hear
    my experiences by my reading some poems

Those types of engagements may be the kind that put my addiction
    to rest so I can finally heal
Some concept that is, and really an idea, but I wonder how I
    would feel?

To be able to guide others and, in doing so, be able to finally own
    up to my addiction's past
Right now I'm not too sure how to make this happen, or if it did,
    how long I could make it last

Helping others as a service is shadowed by my finally owning my
    past, helps me a million times over
My disease just had its 30-year birthday. Could all the pain and
    hurt from my past be my four-leafed clover?

Addict Is Me

Lately, life has given me so much to think about, so where should
I begin?
Guess I should start with a tidbit from my past and where I have
been

One look into my eyes tells you a familiar story; a troubled life
complicated with addiction
As if getting through life is not hard enough without this awful
affliction

Watch my movement, my ticks, and my body language. They also
will tell you the tale
Unsettled and standoffish, uncomfortable and jumpy from a 30-
year battle in Hell

Take a gander at my skin, the pick marks, and the scars on my
face so prevalent, so many
If I happen to talk to you or possibly feature a smile, if you were
looking for teeth, don't bother. There aren't any

If you see me on the street, it must mean I am out of jail, but
probably still not actually free
Before then, take some advice that I did not. If you have an
addiction, it's never too late to find help. Just don't end up like
me.

Compulsion

As I sit here and push my pen across the page
It occurs to me I had better change
Think it would have come to me before this stage
Trapped behind these prison walls, turn the page

A couple of things now come to mind
First, the striking reality of my life resting upon a judge's gavel
Next, what have I done to make my community and my family
    proud?
Disturbing that I'm the problem inside me, no matter how far I
    try to run or travel
If I could simply listen to my past and the silent screams so loud

Then maybe I could give this schizophrenic a future, a breath of
    peace and hope
In looking back, thirty years now the addict, that seems to be the
    hardest task
Twenty-eight of those years seeking refuge and solace from a
    bottle and a bag of dope
On my knees now, I beg you, Lord, take this compulsion from me
    forever. Is that too much to ask?

Lastly

The sun has set upon my life, no tomorrow
Time to leave the past, the present, all my sorrow
Give back emotion, my soul, I stole or borrowed

So dead inside in life, it is me I mourn
Can no longer wait 'til judge and jury are adjourned
Gladly lay down all I know and that I have learned

Cannot change my hair or change my name
Can't build new dreams without the shame
My life was a living hell, I could not get tamed

Press my head into my open palms
Try for a moment to figure out what's going on
I hear the angels singing clearly and beautifully now
Singing Loren's song

Danger without the Riddles

I have written so very much in here
And have said so little, wow!

My words in here blur together and seem to have no clout
Who will I be when I leave the walls of this facility?
Who will I seek when I need to pout?
What will I do when I need to shout?

Those being the questions I ask
My future, from then and now
I feel these are the poignant ones to ask
Without a doubt

As I sit and ponder, I think and wonder
If I will do what is right, mind, body, soul
Or will I make the same mistakes
For it's me I rape if I prove I have learned nil, zero point squat

Do I need to be beaten and spanked into submission, a life so
    paltry?
Or will I break this pattern of nonsense, no time left, I realize
    now, in my life to be faulty!
I have a new mindset this time and its root is one all can count on
And I have no doubt in me, nor should none question

Just a few points now: leave the state if allowed, get my life back
    on track, mental health
On my meds to make me stable as I was before, making all around
    me safe and myself and family proud!
To take a hard good look at me, ever closer than ever before,
    proving to all I'll do the work without hesitation
No gamble at all because I am already gone, heading in that
    direction!

I will be stepping far away from anger, the selfish acts and people
    that brought me behind these forsaken walls
And into the honorable judge's chambers
I will be bringing a sober me along with my words of experience
    and my poems to the world
To remind me where I've been, delivering them to those who still
    suffer

I will do what I can to give a helping hand to all those with
    addictions and psychoses, whether by speech or my poems
Hopefully giving someone peace and hope for their restless soul
On my soapbox, even if my words are heard only by me or a
    perfect stranger
Sharing my thoughts of paranoia and abuse and the feelings of
    impending doom
The addiction, the fear, the ever-present danger

Hope's Conveyor

Erased a thought
Often forgot
Feelings for naught
A chase I fought

Coins tossed
A gambler's loss
Friends crossed
Getting sauced

Life's wink
Eye's stink
Morning drink
No time to think

Smack the ground
Few turn around
Falling down
No hallowed ground

Never enough
Knees scuffed
Hands cuffed
Life muffed

Wonder why
Deep sigh
Dreams die
Eyes cry

Peel back layers
Time for prayer
Hope's conveyor
Bottle slayer
Jesus is life's purveyor

My Way

That unwelcome friend is coming around again
I barricade my doors and it still gets in

These boundaries crossed lead to such misery
Then I am not who I am supposed to be

Beat up, pinned down, and shut out
Lost in the mayhem is what living's about

Dragged down by my ball and chain
Blanketed emotions, feeling no pain

Lord, could tomorrow be the day
On which you save me, my way?

Mountain High

A dream way atop on a mountain high
With the naked eye, not a cloud in the sky

Aesthetically universal perfection above and below
Obvious the answers I ask for are now certainly known

Pillars of strength not made of dirt and stone
For the mountain I climbed was me
The beauty I saw was me leaving my fears all alone

Keyhole Soul

Eerie shadows tickle the darkness, yet no one is found
My eyes, my breath and chest are the only motion around

Stoic I stand, while fear is driving the life from me
Has the Angel of Death finally come to lay his claim to thee?

I stifle terroristic screams welling up deep from my core
Now my only chance to survive is to find and run for the door

My eyes are wide open, yet I can't see my hand in front of my face
Quickly I say a prayer to God "Please Lord, get me out of this
    place"

Then I realize the demonic shadows are fragments of my soul,
    broken
Separated from me by the darkness in my heart, my mind, and by
    the words I've spoken

I couldn't find a door to exit this place, but I located a key and a
    keyhole
The only way to leave and to piece my soul back together is to
    follow the lead of spiritual people

The Wave

Ride the wave of life and dream
Carve a path where no others have been

Set a standard beyond example
Thirst for knowledge, there is more than ample

Be the one who jumps into the rare air of the limelight
Show you care to those around when something's not right

Take an oath of spirituality
One of no posterity

Ride the wave of life, be driven in a positive direction
Ride the wave of life away from the influences of addiction

Me

Me,
   I am starting to see
   Head out of the clouds
   Screaming so loud now
   Can I let me be me?

Me,
   I'm not really this guy
   Who will pray to the sky
   'Til I'm so raked into the ground
   Dirt is up to my eyes

Me,
   I am starting to see, hoping after all
   I can refrain from my next fall
   And enjoy this thing
   Life is allowing me to see

Go

My confusion is nothing at all that is new
I've built my life, for 30 years now, solely around you

Times of angst and pain when you promised to comfort me
Now in reality, I'm terrified, alone. It's only me I see

I can't live without you or leave you behind
My friend, we've been together a long, long time

Together, a promise of dying is all I see, and that we both know
Thanks anyway for being there for so long, but I have to let you go

Karma

I rise to the circumstance to execute my given purpose
Desperation is no longer a resolution to my endless searches

My actions give birth to my present and future experiences
Through ongoing mental enhancement, I will create and condition
    a spiritual and positive flow

Paving my way toward enlightenment
And a path for that positive flow, karma, to grow

I will commit to no longer hurting myself or anyone with my
    mind, body, or speech
Saving myself and others from suffering by the ways and thoughts
    and negatives I preach

I will consider others and help them grow in their minds and in
    their hearts
The ceaseless benefit of others will be my priority when each day
    ends and another one starts.

Let It Go

When I ride atop a cloud above the fire of the dragon's breath
A barrel roll and a fall from grace ensues, then I plummet to
    certain death

As I thread the needle to stitch the time in and out, it plunges
    crimson red
A seamstress less a pattern to follow, by design clothing to be worn
    when dead

When wearing those glasses, viewing life through the bottles, it's
    me I can't see
I need a change of fashion and style to bring me back to date, or
    my eulogy I'll soon read

Chase the kitty or take a ride on the horse, the Black Stallion
I will end up all alone without a God or friend to help me fend off
    the addiction battalion

Go your own direction. Remember, though, some must die so
    others may live
So without resentment I'm going along with my higher power and
    serenity, my friend
Don't forget to let it go! And pray as well as forgive!

Tried

I am running a race I had not conditioned for, one of forced
    sobriety
So used to running on my own agenda and all caught up in
    self-notoriety

Now behind these walls of this institution, loneliness and fear the
    overwhelming feeling
Guilt is closing the walls in on me, as I'm crushed by my shame's
    ceiling

Gone now are all those people who said they would always be
    there to help me
That is the result I have manifested, because in my life, I use and I
    am all about me

I am getting old and very tired of me destroying my life and others
    with my addiction
Look closely, my nerves are all exposed like I'm inside out, this
    battle of attrition

To those whom I have failed and to those I and my selfishness
    have cast aside
When I die, and it may not be long if I use again, put on my
    headstone "Loren, an addict who tried"

Epiphany

Blood, bone, flesh, living beings, God's tests
Now gasping and gulping for each essential breath

Inaudible sounds, fist hits the ground
A shattered rear-view mirror shows a broken past, a road with only
    me around

Sun's warming comfort and light
Disappears, swallowed by every new night

Gone are its rays when the moon has its way
Also when cloud's shadows flooded April's wash away the flowers
    blossom seed for May

It's with a fist pump of victory
A blossom's seed becomes what it's intended to be

Then I look once again into the mirror
And that's when I notice I'm alive, I am me, and I am OK, and
    that's my epiphany

The Re-direct

To Mother and Father for the love you have given
You took my pathetic life and now I am driven

What is now in my heart I could have never obtained
With the blackness I came with life would not have sustained

I feel blessed by your mature strength and power
I can face the world now and not have to cower

Before I came here I lost hope of me healing
Then you poured out your souls with love as the feeling

Thank you so for your sacrifice and that is for sure
The challenges ahead I'm sure I can endure

My Distraction

I don't use lots of big words
Why is that so absurd?

I keep my maximum syllables to three
For beyond that, I don't know any

When I write a sentence to a poem
I feel I am the audience and I better show 'em

Connections of experience and thought
Complicated by life's battles I have fought

Uncertain that any of my poems are good
But it's me giving me attention, that is understood

Putting my word to page helps me and others understand
The walk I have taken thus far across this land

When I read them, I get all kinds of reactions
The how, the what, the why, and the OMG Loren! like I'm the
    coming attraction

If I told you just one thing about it that I enjoy
It keeps me from hurting any longer, as it is one hell of a great
    distraction!

Goodbye

Hold me, now kiss me goodbye
Don't you see, we really tried

Walk away, so that I may shine
Leave and go forever this time

Been with you each night and day
But now I believe I'll be OK

Go become a star in another's sky
With you I know I can never fly

We've beat this drum before as a ritual
For me this time it is personal

Can't you see that I really tried?
Go now! No more kisses goodbye

Mind

A million times I have fought your ways, but you are so inviting
Giving in to you has always been easier than the pain of fighting

Each victory of yours, you gnash your teeth and sink them deeper
into my bones
Giving you more control over me, the thoughts of you never leave
me alone

In all my times of emotional and physical hunger, you fed my needs
Evil, you chew at the underbelly of my soul, sowing fields of
hopelessness, your demonic seeds

Piece by piece, day to day, your blackness has blanked my life
from anything good
Freely I gave to you my everything, my family, my dignity, my soul,
all I could

30 years of having nothing. Looking back, there is nothing good
to find
I leave you now where you took me. I leave now with my fear,
hope, and God, and what you've left of my mind

Follow Me

A place so familiar, yet it is a place that I have never been
With smells so new, yet so close to my recollection every now and
again

When I listen closely, I am amazed at all the wonderful sounds.
They are music to my ears
Almost sensual, erotic, the feeling of each and every object that I
touch. Weird!

Colors are so vivid and so bright to my eyes and all that I see
I savor each taste of this place I'm at right now. It's amazing, come
on with me

Odd, but comforting, that I am feeling again things I had lost
when I gave up on sobriety and me

Dream, I Have*

Two score and five years ago
In California, an American addict there was born
For many years and for many people, his momentous disease did
    not show
Until society's flames of justice rooted him by his thorn

Forty-five years have come to pass, chances of freedom and
    integrity
Through selfish will, exiled himself, acts of social treason
Dramatized herein is nothing, to all it's plain to see
A perpetual foundation of diseased living, season upon season

The progressively crippling nature of this lonely, shameful
    condition
Was unforeseen when our forefathers wrote the Constitution and
    Declaration of Independence
All Americans now fall heir, charged for their lives not coming to
    fruition
Black and white, women and men, children and adults all
    vulnerable to chemical dependence

As addicts we have defaulted on our sacred pursuit of happiness
Defaulted on an open check written, one of freedom and liberty
We give in to our demon knowingly with explosive and impulsive
    gladness
Consequences rendered of bludgeoned ethics, leaving in their
    wake morals that destroy society

Now is the time to fight to live, we must rise now against our disease
Now is the time to fight for an end to our suffering as God's children
Now is the time for us and our families to get up off our bloody
    knees
Now is the time to alleviate strain on America and to lighten your
    burden

Further, it would be fatal for the addicted not to achieve sobriety's freedom

Yet futile for the wheels of justice not to challenge your addiction's healing plight

Through the whirlwinds of your revolt you will locate inner peace and justice's kingdom

However weary, my fellow addicts, work the steps, continue to fight

So great will you and your America become along your offensive with newly found sobriety

As what was the you of old slides deeper into your tragic history's past

As you lay flower petals of hope, you walk down sidewalks of new dreams in society

Gathering strength where once there was not a single victory to last

Once begun, we must remain vigilant, never to become complacent nor satisfied

We need to remember how long it took for us to get sick, and then to have enough

We must reflect upon the spiritual pains of emptiness and the tears we cried

We must get back on and ride, even when we fall down and life gets tough

Through remembering our difficulties prior to today and tomorrow

Addicts can lay down our vices and rejoin society as welcomed equals

Through service, faith, and hope, better choices will be made, guiding us further from sorrow

Catching wind for our wings, like the ocean's breeze frees a flying gull

I have a dream, where once upon a time
I merely had a dream
Let sobriety ring
Let sobriety ring

★ *Inspired by Martin Luther King's "I Have A Dream" speech*

CLIMBING UP FROM THE DEPTHS

No More

No hand to lift me from above
No one left to give me love
All alone in life, I'm terrified
So scared, I can't remember why I cry

Daddy taught me to buck up
Momma told me life's rough
My moral standing has run aground
I'm slipping away without a sound

I fear each day to see the morning light
Another day alive, I don't have the fight
Must get myself to the end of my rainbow
Go big and make the news so everyone will know

My blue eyes are now bloodshot red
Life's too heavy for my head
God take my soul home, lift me off the floor
Lord, please understand, my heart can take no more

Mercy

As a last resort, I drop to my knees and put my hands together
I bow my head into my hands and close my eyes, attempting to do
    it right
Shut tight, I then call unto my Lord and Savior in prayer, Jesus
    Christ

Hey Lord, it's me again and it has been a while, and as you know,
    I'm in trouble
I pray to you now, my Lord, hoping your blessing is delivered on
    the double
Please don't wait until my meager foundation crumbles further to
    rubble

I realize I only cry out to you when I can absolutely take no more
I also realize how difficult it's been for me to make time to walk
    through your door
Lord, I'm really tired of living and I need my wings now to lift my
    soul from the floor

I know I can't enter heaven if I take my life with my own hands
So with great respect, I beg your tender mercy, my Lord. End my
    life now, so I may enter the King's land

Prison

Prison has stripped my soul beyond the grasp of fancy and that of
    freedom's passion
Surfacing tumultuous emotive reactions from within me, prior
    never in fashion

Skillfully chiseled footprints chosen so as not to get caught in the
    tawdry spider's web
Then life, with utter disregard for my enchantment, watched the
    flow intercede and tackle the ebb

Bunyan and ox would not accept the challenge to reseed the fruit
    of my dignity with plow to till
Nay, at a count greater each of a hundred to break of my spirit, my
    hope, or my will

Reaper of your most grim fruits, the wretched seed you have sown
    shall surely poison all in time
And the poetic words delivered at your eulogy with a smile as wide
    as a piano face will no doubt be mine

Show Me

What's in a word?
Can you show me?

What's in a name?
Can you show me?

Am I alone?
Can you show me?

How can I grow?
Can you show me?

Why am I here?
Can you show me?

How can I forgive?
Can you show me?

What's the right way to live?
Can you show me?

Who can I turn to?
Can you show me?

Who truly loves me?
Can you show me?

Whose promise is never broken?
Can you show me?

What does life have planned?
Can you show me?

What does peace mean?
Can you show me?

How can I find love?
Can you show me?

What can I do to live free?
Can you show me?

How do I let you in?
Can you show me?
Where do I go to find you, Jesus
     Christ, my Lord?
Can you show me?

Selfish Things

Today, I went down to the old wishing well
Tossed in a nickel and asked God for my family's health

When I was younger, I wished for very selfish things
Like all the stuff unlimited money could bring

I went to that well with a pocket full of coins
Tossed one in and wished for a beauty to satisfy my loins

Pitched another one in and asked for a bad-ass car
Right behind that, I threw another and requested a rare guitar

Then, to save time, I threw those nickels in two at a time
The cost per throw and two wishes made was a dime

Soon enough my pocket was empty and I felt like a fool
Always trying to buy the easy way to happiness, so not cool

If my wishes were prayers instead and my coins represented spirituality
I would still have my coins, and by now, God would have answered me

Untitled

An impenetrable trembling, the fever

Aghast at the mysteries and shadows of darkness

A terrific horror floats in on the wind

Waking a horror, evident on the faces of the once placid and blissful

Skin crawls with its ripples, chilling waves from head to toe

Faint tortured breath breezes closer in path from where, still I do not know

"For Heaven's sake! Not now!" I scream internally

"Don't make me pay with my soul all at once!" A deal made with the demon

"Give me one more chance to repent to Him, My Lord, less my unruly treason!"

An impulsive cry of fear seated on the vehicle of impending doom's evil scornful sister, karma and reality

Swiftly, I run out from the shadow's eerie darkness toward my Lord and Savior's light, away from Hell's bottomless gravity

Wounded Knees

I know you have been there for others through thick and thin
But now it's me, Lord, who cries out for you to confess my sins

Oh Father, my will has run riot and my spiritual contempt and
  lack of control unabashed
My bondage I am carrying with me so heavy, I feel each breath
  may be my last

I am on wounded knees now, and I am begging and praying to
  you, my Lord, seeking forgiveness
Will you fill my heart with your spirit and love, Jesus Christ as my
  witness?

Sultan's Tavern

Driven into sultan's tavern, the feeling of a shadowless soul held in death's contempt

Escaping the dungeon of doom impossible now, its fiery walls hold the living's passed on soulless faces within; no reprieve by your eternal master; do not attempt

Enslaved by Satan now, the mindless delivered themselves unto him over and over again into the depths of evil's dark abyss with every mortal sin

The place below has a cell for all of us; doom and a soulless afterlife can certainly be gotten without following His ten commandments

In life may you allow His divine spirit to heal you, for His is the power, the honor, and the glory "King" and with Him, make your mark through prayer and repent!

Defeats

After so many debilitating and devastating personal defeats
This addict's anger, fears, and depression have knocked me from
    my feet

Now I seek shelter through enlightenment, a release from the
    bondage of my disease's pain
Heavenly Father, humbly, through my spiritual awakening, I ask
    for the ability to abstain

Lord, I pray now for your tender mercy to bestow a miracle within
    my heart
Jesus Christ, my Lord and Savior, I pray tomorrow for my sobriety
    to start

King

It is in the good book, so take some time, read, and take a long look
Men have often taken greater men and abandoned them in prison
As a way to persecute or to circumvent an act of faith to an ideal
As a way to thwart a secular way of thought or good intent

The gathering of all man's forces
To tragically corral this wayward man without any horses
A man who often traveled alone, never claiming a home
Was beaten down as he traveled town to town
As he tried to speak, often no love shown
By the cities and townships and all around the super power, at the
    time being Rome

He, the King, carried nothing and cared not of possession
The many doubters became few, post resurrection
How many a perfect soul has passed since or before
That showed the entire world about love, not a bit about greed
And would, in greeting you for the first time, drop to their knees
    to wash your feet?

Two thousand plus years now passed, no one like Him now or before
Gethsemane proves to all that Jesus is Lord and King of all kin
By taking on the atonement of man and accepting in selfless
    abandonment the sufferance of every man's sin

Untitled

Welcome to our world, the Virgin Mother says to her new born son
Just take your first breath and your life has truly begun

Relieved, at one journey's end while another comes to rise
Brings tears of joy to Mary, the prize bearer's eyes

Truly a gift to all who have "drank of the cup" and believe in Him
Performing miracles as was His atonement of suffering for man's sin

From clay-formed birds taking true life form and flight
To the blind, upon His healing, tender touch, receiving sight

My Lord and Savior always is with me, for I am never scared or alone
With the spirit of Jesus Christ where I lay my head, that is my home

Clouds

Beyond the darkness of each passing night
I set my soul to sail free, to take flight
At that time, there is no wrong or right
I am free to breathe again, less the judgment plight

There, I rise above the suffering crowd
Above the trapped voices that scream so loud
Without the guilt of those I've made unproud
For my king's throne is there among the clouds

Resurrection Day

In my next life, I get to be the world's hero
You get to be the one who is the lifelong addicted
If resurrected, I would be elated with the role reversal
Imprisoned internally, and in and out of jail. A soul, a life,
    adjudicated

I want to be the one fortune always chases
Not the one who is never noticed or ever missed
You get to hide through masks with pock-marked faces
You can only imagine being the one the Lord had blessed

I can only dream of the comfort and beauty of being truly loved
To be the one with the beautiful body and the amazing mind
Give to you the stigma of being the one God kicked and shoved
Or the one told by everyone all his life, "you are not our kind"

I want to be the member of society, the father, son, brother, friend,
    who is always trusted
I pray each day, in every way, that tomorrow is my resurrection day

Enough said

Round and Round

Round and Round
You are my hell and your control turns my life upside down

Round and Round
You got hold of me and kicked me all around

Round and Round
You took me as a child. Now I'm 30 years your clown

Round and Round
You chase my soul from town to town

Round and Round
My king and queen, you have always worn the crown

Round and Round
You damaged me so badly, I can't ever be unwound

Round and Round
You took away my smile. Now I only frown

Round and Round
You have died in me, now that God I have found

Give Your Soul To Jesus

Give your soul to Jesus
He is the one to help you heal
Free you from your numbness and to make you feel

Give your soul to Jesus
You won't need to pick up a phone
Or ever will you go alone

Give your soul to Jesus
His powers are amazing, true, and legit
Demons within self simply forfeit

Give your soul to Jesus
Pray, kneel, get on your knees
His is the gateway, spiritual freedom, and all-knowing
King's love is yours, don't forget

Give your soul to Jesus

Testify

I testify now to the spirit and incredible power of my Lord and Savior

I testify now my personal relationship with Jesus Christ is far beyond the value of any treasure

I testify now His kingdom of Peace and Joy will be delivered unto you through prayer in quantities unimaginable and in ways you cannot measure

I testify now Jesus Christ will set you free, releasing your soul from the bondage accumulated in life and which it has tethered

I testify now that Jesus Christ is my Lord and my Savior and as I walk with Him, I am no longer alone or afraid in this life or my afterlife, giving my life peace and love I sought, with forgiveness at heart, bringing my existence on Earth its most pleasure

My Path

My path is lit by Jesus Christ
My Lord and Savior shows me I will be alright
Spiritually embattled I have been all of my life
Until recently I called upon Him and asked Him to keep me in
    His sights

I'm a man of sin
Seems to never end
When I call His name again
He forgives me for my trend
Always lets me in
Allows my broken spirit to mend

My path is lit by Jesus Christ
My Lord and Savior shows me I will be alright
If I take a little time to pray
My fears will quickly go away
I will make it through another day

My path is lit by Jesus Christ

My Soul's Wings

Humbly, I ask this of you, my Lord, my Savior, Jesus Christ
At my life's end, give my soul wings to take flight

So it may fly to all the lives in need and guide them to you, Lord,
    and a better way
Giving the weak enough strength to make it through another day
Allowing the mute a voice in life and giving them a say

Easing those who are in fear, building their courage to battle on
Righting all of those in the world who have ever been done wrong

Lord, hear my prayer so I may help the sick, the old, the hungry,
    the poor
Help them find you as I have, my Lord, so that they will suffer no
    more

Perfect, Like Him

I found forgiveness for my sins
Through my beliefs in and of Him

He lights my path I walk each day
His purpose guides each step along the way

With Him I am never scared or alone
My home and heart is my neighbor's home at heart

Thank you dearly, Jesus Christ, Lord and Savior
For your spirit, my life, and love's flavor

I thank you for your tender mercy
Releasing me from bondage, setting me free

I shall guide others humbly to you
From one day's end 'til forever, anew

Shh!

Pursed lips
Against death's fingertip

Soul pulled
Leaves body icy cold

Judas fit
Too much to forget

One desire
Smolders in the fire

Wit's end
Satan's grip starts again

Prayed wish
Deity and sacred bliss

Release from
Under the reaper's thumb

God's door
I will be found once more

Deity

I want to thank you, Lord, for giving me a new beginning
A reprieve from a distasteful past and a mind conditioned for sinning

Now in my life, I take you with me and I do not worry
I keep your song in my heart and an even pace. I'm in no hurry

Lord, thank you for allowing me into your deity, your shining light
Thank you, Jesus, for your sacrifice and guiding me to the path of
    right

Now your spirit lives in me through your forgiveness and my faith
Not sure how I made it so long without giving glory to God, and
    you my praise

LOVE

Blessing

You are a blessing from the heavens above
Brought to me in truth, beauty, and love

Day in and day out, of you I can never get enough
My heart has beat solely for you since our very first touch

At that moment, you set my soul afire
Burning and yearning so deeply, fueled by passionate desires

I think about you only, my mind won't stop
Mental images of sexy you and that body you rock

Many times I have felt like I am dreaming and I ask, how can it be?
As if once I was totally blind and you gave me a gift, a vision to see

Moonlit and star-filled nights give way reluctantly to the next day's sun
Even so, it feels as though our night's love has just begun

You save me, and you are all I have ever needed, and I still do
You are my soul mate, my universe, my everything, so very true

I thank you for being you and I need you to understand
You have taught me all I know about love, and about being a man

My Dream Woman

Beautiful long hair, black as a moonless night's darkest horizon

Eyes of blue-green, warm and inviting as the Mediterranean Sea

Skin so fair and sweet, like fine silk mixed perfectly with
buttermilk cream

Graceful touch, elegant and precise, like the most-skilled diamond
cutter

Smells as wonderful as a grove of eagerly blooming May flowers
aside a mountain's stream

Presence of a well-traveled and worldly education, aristocratic queen

Speaks as if her voice's sound were delivered by the Lord's angels
themselves

Anyway

I have one thing left that I want to say
So I am very glad you called to tell me you are going away

Even though I had hoped for better news for us today
I am certain that at some point I will be OK

Stay true to your dreams and don't get tangled up in the fray
I say this all the while trying to keep my tears at bay

Pick up the phone sometime, call, even just to say "Hey!"
Always remember you are more beautiful than all the flowers in
    May

Even brighter and hotter than all the sun's rays
I wish you well in all your life's ventures, all of your days

Although I'm confused, I know you deserve better than me anyway

Worthy

Am I worthy of your love? If so, how can it be?
After each fall and every shove. Me? What do you see?

Better look again, or pray above I project constructive apathy
Really, it fits you and me like a glove. Contrived, I am not who
you see

Worthy of your love?
Sure, if I were not affected and all about me

Another Level

You are levels above all of the natural wonders of heaven
God's most beautiful of creations, adding one to the seven

Known or imagined in dreams, none greater, future, present, or past
Angels are jealous. Wistful, envious eyes they cast

Purity's goblet nourishes my thirst of your soul. I drink
Captive wonderment, astounding manner in which you think

Mirror linked hearts, arm in arm, hands, fingers interlacing
Bountiful treasure troves, two blend into one, galacticly embracing

Timeless jewels universe eyes depths sparkle like stars
Eloquence complimenting heavenly bounds from near and far

Disbelief, the honor agreed her choice sealed at altar
Tragic, nothing would befall the next moment if we were to falter

Pursed lips the space between two lovers there had breached
Filling my bosom with love of life once allowed leached

Doubts, fears became lame, moot their word then on
Demonic loneliness, the mouse within this now man long since gone

Sparkle my eyes cast upon god's most beautiful angel
Forever my soul's love knot, yours to keep or untangle

Second Sight

I long for our time together
To let the world witness our sparks, day or night

When I get to prove to you, if for only one moment
The fire that burns in me for you, wrong or right

From the time that my eyes first caught yours in passing 'til now
Ever longing to bring them together once again, second sight

This yearning I have for you so deeply ingrained in me, so true. It
     is ever consuming my soul
My eyes' only desire is to once again embrace your presence and
     witness your beauty. If given this chance, my life would be
     whole

Lying awake after we kiss goodnight

To marvel your beauty gracing the moonlight

An ending, fruitless treasure hunt's plight

Love's jewel trove of what's right

Infinite euphoria until eternity's last starry night

Revolving around your life, love's satellite

Blown mind, body-rocking dynamite

Swollen heart famously found its limelight

If blinded, our love's my eyesight

American queen from her noble knight

Thank you for the soul mate's copyright

The Lord, The You, The Me

"The Lord, The You, The Me"
  As witnessed; an event;
Given by God, surreal and parallel
  Awestruck by life, by hope, by love
Fell; a single droplet of water
  Descent ended; accumulative with
Alike. A new beginning.
  Mirrored, a placid pool;
Waters unmolested.
  Landing, emanating a wake;
Ripples of life's energy, at center
  A destination's end..
Boundless, anew –
  As witnessed; an event
An essential motor; my heart
  A vehicle; my body, my soul
Given by God;
  My ears, the sound; veins
My nectar; The coursing of
  Through miles of byways;
A beating; pounding loudly,
  Knocking outwardly; audible
The inside a drum...
  The parallel; surreal
Droplets wake; a breath of movement;
  Living across the water
My soul, my heart;
  A longing for you, your love.
My chest; every single beat;
  Water's shore, my body; Alive
Impossible to contain; outward
  Expression of internal desire;
Fuel from you; from me; allowed
  If so by God; our love

Alone

I want to be kissed and loved as if I am needed
I want to be a part of someone whom love has seeded

I want to laugh and wander through a conversation all night talking
I want to be held under a moonlit night while meanderingly walking

I want to stay up way too late so my day is absurd
I want to make love and be made love to without a single word

I want someone who builds their days and nights around me
I want to know if true love exists, because alone, I'm all I see

Comfort

Eyes desire burn with the hottest flame

A white-hot blue glows within my dream

Culprit of my breath, victim am I to your game

Until intersecting paths parallel, to your love I am a fiend

A bright sun poised to reach above the arch of a newly lit horizon

Gives hope to the new day in which I shall find you near

Within my vision's grasp, you are more beautiful than any have laid eyes on

May this day's night find my head resting comfortably upon your breast with nothing left in life for me to want or fear

Dream Girl

Honey, when you looked at me and smiled
Your cat-like eyes drove me wild

I knew right then I had to have you
Never before or since had I seen a woman so beautiful, it's true

Baby, let me lay my jacket over a puddle
I would marry you just to simply cuddle

Goin' to call my Momma and tell her about my new best friend
Tell my Pops my very lonely heart is now on the mend

Goin' to two-step on down this new path of life
With my dream girl at my side, everything's goin' to be all right
Got my friend to cuddle, got my friend to hold me tight

Girl, you know just who you are
I wished for you upon a zillion falling stars

Everything is finally goin' to be all right
Got my best friend to hold me tight

Winds of Change

A windy event with clear skies before the rain
Two lovers aboard the ship, one crazy, one sane
I put you on an island alone with so much disdain
With a mind made so heavy from words full of pain

I've lied to eyes of my past and also my heart
All so perilous journeys right from the start
For now I see your true beauty, funny and smart
Much more than before we were ever apart

We are sure to see turbulent and rough seas ahead
I promise this to you, girl. I will never see red
You are my one, this I know until I am dead
And I miss hearing you love me as you often once said

To Mom: Beautiful Wings

I want to know how to find you, Mom, at my life's end
What if I am on the other side of the gate and can't get in?

Surely you will be greeted by God's angels and given your own set
of beautiful wings
How will I know you are OK if God says Heaven's not really my
sort of thing?

It makes me so terribly sad to realize one day our mortal lives will end
I am so scared not to be good enough to be with you, Mom, when
afterlife begins

To Have and To Hold

May the fire that burns between us light our path to eternal love
May the respect we give to each other never dwindle or come to
    push and shove

May laughter and joy fill each moment of our lives, bringing us
    eternal bliss
May ever our time apart be short, for your soul I surely would miss

May we, together, forever share tender moments we each would
    never forget
May we make one wish at life's end to live us again and again to
    heart's content

May we allow each day to begin with a shared smile from its very start
May we complete one another in each and every way, allowing
    love's spirit into our hearts

May we truly have love's magic warming each other forever, soul
    to soul
May you hold me now in your arms until I pass, and me you, to
    have and to hold

Time Machine

Girl, when I think about your love, I hunger for you with the most
voracious appetite
For you feed me what I need, and it's your loving I can never get
enough of, day or night

Walk with me down life's wonderful path, hand in hand together
forever, enjoying one another's stride
When I watch you, I learn so much. You complete me, give me
strength, and make me feel so alive

With you at my side, I truly feel that life is magical, and I know I
have found life's beautiful treasure
You bring my life, my world, the most endearment and joy beyond
love's wildest imagination and pleasure

There is not a single thing I would change about you. If I could, it
would be a sin
With a matchmaking time machine, I would choose you, how you
are, all over again!

Come

Why has the love in my heart never truly been withstanding?
Was it temporary like a season? Did I lack greater understanding?

Did the tectonic plates not shift or the planetary stars align?
Have I reached the point, for what it's worth, best to remain benign?

Naturally of each the four seasons is not the one we love
Blended, eased gently one to the next, not ushered in by knee-jerk
    shove

As so it should be in love as the seasons same should transpire
Immersed slowly to begin, in time bathed completely with
    burning desire

Shall love forever remain just beyond my reach's grasp?
Trickery, my maker's game of hide and seek, behind lock and hasp

Undaunted, I will seek the world over 'til eyes are black and blue
Oath, I will settle for nothing less than contentment, love being
    true

For just as seasons refuse to last, yet another is still to come
With the change upon us, may my soul find its only one

Coffee

Her daily vigor feeds my soul, that of an almost tar

For without her fueling my being, surely I'd not get far

Oils atop her ebony darkness purse my anxious lips

An unexplainable emotion, her aroma quells shaky finger tips

Once inside, she warms me as if wrapped in a fuzzy blanket

A day without her goodness, I think I could not make it

Throughout the day she is with me, habitually it would seem

I know if I went without her, I'd truly run out of steam

Terminal Love

Love is only criminal
If it's not the kind that's terminal

Words free-floated as if they were on clearance at a market
Bang! Boo! Pow! Gone are those who said them as quickly as the
spark hit

Isn't love supposed to be a passage of two into a dimension beyond
a door?
Not the kind that leaves a trail of broken heart pieces beyond
repair upon the floor

Shouldn't love stand the storm of any type of weather?
Or is it so devalued by selfishness that is flushed away at the drop
of a feather?

Would it all be love if it were consummated beyond the words
promised on the altar?
Could love's spirit survive each time in those relations without falter?

Does love judge one's motive as a way of saying "I've had it this time?"
Is love a passage of rights that in the end are drawn on a page,
what's yours, what's mine?

Will love slip through your hands the tighter you try to hold onto it?
Compassion and empathy the exception, not the rule, when we
fail to embrace and cuddle it

I've learned a lot about love and why it's been said to me "it's terminal"
Because I never had it at all unless it was me loving the ideas, the
tough, and physical

Take Me

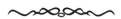

I built my glass house all around you, and now I am no use
Tried to climb beyond your walls when I noticed your ruse

You came to me when I was weak and had nothing to lose
Now you are a part of each breath I take, mine and also fools
Always changing me, killing me, breaking moral boundaries and
   rules

Ever since we first met and you planted your hateful demon seed
My world has surrounded yours but I'm the one left in need

I can't ever imagine letting you go. Who will I then be?
I'd have no idea how to live healthy without you, it's you I feed
Can't let you go, my life is all about you, what I feel, what I see

My love is about dancing with you in my hand, in the candlelight
Because when you dance with me, you make me feel all right

Honey, take me away right now, you know where I want to go tonight
Away from here, girl, anywhere with you, anytime together baby,
   out of sight

Sun's Heart

Sun is going down
There is no one around

Just you and me
Looking out at the sea

Got my baby doll on my lap
So sexy, bikini top, jean shorts, ball cap

Going to roll this day into night
Holding my baby doll tight

Setting sun reflects in her eyes
Her heart matches its size

Brushing her hair from her face, I give her a kiss
Bringing on the night, nothing could be better than this

Snow Angel

Baby, can you give me your word that you will always need me?
I swear your needs will always be heard

I will always remember when we met so long ago
Amazing that through time how my love for you still grows

From our first conversation that first time we spoke on the phone
My heart has been yours and only yours all alone

So many firsts that I still look back on and smile when remembered
Like our first cold-lipped kiss that snowy walk we took in December

Making angels in the snow white, still holding one another's hand
Showing the world that New Year's party, this is my woman and
    I'm her man

And just when I thought life could never get any sweeter than this
We were given the Lord's blessing and had 3 beautiful kids

All these years later and so many firsts still to reach for and touch
All these years later, and I still love you so very much

Shine, My Star

You are a beautiful woman, both from near and afar
You are amazing at all you do, so well above par
You are the most brilliant example of a shining star
So don't change a single thing about you or who you are

You have already proven that, for me, you are right
You have no competition, no one or reason to fight
You are essential to my dreams and to all my days and nights
You've put an end to my searches for the one to hold tight

You always, with class and respect, say the right things
You uncloud my eyes and relieve my life's pains
You wash away a history of relationships and loveless stains
Please keep me at your side, lover, but never in vain

Pot Of Gold

Let's get out and go somewhere we have never been
Pack some clothes, get our poles, and our wet-nosed furry friends

We'll hop in that old truck and roll those windows all the way down
Get off the highway and find some dirt road way out of town

It's time for us to get away and put down life's boxing gloves
Get back to what is important and what put us in love

Like being together and exploring some far away remote place
Get away from all the pressures of life, leave the hellish rat race

Put your hand in mine and I will not let go. You are my pot of gold
You know I love you loving me, so let's let it show and be told

We have worked so hard and earned this time for just you and me
Let's play, drink, camp, laugh, and feel our love again, maybe even
    climb a tree

My Color

White is the color of angelic purity that I see in you

Green is the color of life's growth between me and you

Yellow is the color of the friendship I have with you

Blue is the color of my soul when I'm not with you

Red is the color my heart's blood, loving you

Black would forever be my color if I ever lost you

Mask

The mask you are wearing each day has been a poor disguise
For the cold I see when I look into your eyes

Seems to me as if you have become emotionally unavailable,
    detached, and gone
Seems like the music in your heart no longer plays our love song

I am not too sure what has brought on this feeling, our crash
Confused and lonely, I look for answers deeply into another empty
    glass

I tried to talk to you and ask you why, long before today
But I was dismissed and you took every opportunity to get away

So just go and don't ever look back, for it's me you will never find
Even if you fall down as the beggar a million and one times

Our relationship has had its final day, and we are its setting sun
Good luck to me, for my perfect, new beginning in life has just
    begun

Star

You feed my heart, fill my empty soul
I pray to hold you forever, never let you go

You always lift me up when I am down
You are my breath when I'm about to drown

You are the most brilliant star in the sky
I need you just to feel alive

You give me hope where there was none
My love for you, unimaginable since it begun

I owe to you a debt of immense gratitude
For saving my life, giving me love, changing my attitude

Love's Paradox

Visually awestruck, combined with the smells of the sweetest
  permeations
Eden's gardens blossom full bloom, bursting with God's creations

Amidst the flawless perfection of a shadowless, moonlit night
In the beginning, two in the image of Him stroll a path along the
  spiritually-guided right

Love's first ever paradox, "Desire" complicates "Beauty", was
  immediately forsaken
Cast away were they forever, unforgiven for not doing as told and
  being contently mistaken

Is It You?

Is it you who will teach this man all about love?

Is it you who will be there when push comes to shove?

Is it you I cry out for in good times and bad?

Is it you who whisks the clouds away for feelings of glad?

Is it you to have and to hold, just me and you?

Is it you 'til eternity's next sunrise is upon us and its day is anew?

Is it you when we are apart whom I long to desperately touch?

Is it you these words were meant for? I love you so much.

Illusions

Probably should have called a prayer in and let you know
I want you to meet me out under our favorite rainbow

There I will be waiting for my beauty in her faded blue jeans
Looking for my queen, the one I see only in my dreams

You appear in my life only during the night
Each moment with you always feels so very right

It happens when I close my eyes and I fall asleep
During the day it is your love that I cannot keep

Why can't I ever really find you or look into your eyes
How come when mine are open you have already said goodbye

It fills my days with such lonely hearted confusion
Us being together only in my nightly dream's illusions

Holding Me

Eyes dazzled by a million stars
Witnessed also are planets Venus and Mars

Breathtaking enormity of the Milky Way
Strewn above the dark horizons that lay

Brilliant falling stars of a meteor shower
I make wish after wish, hour after hour

My first wish was already granted this wonderful night
Hearing you tell me the words "I love you!" while I'm holding you
    tight

Hi

Fluid the imagery caught, unbelievable, with my eyes
Frozen, stunned in concept a dream woman, this guy
Apparition a guess, squinted eyelids, shaking my head side to side

Hair now standing on my neck, skin crawling like it's in a race
She floats towards me true, as one motion of form, precision and
    grace

Unable to speak, for in awe and fighting with literacy's thumbing
    of troubles
Shuffling, I manage to stammer the word "Hi" to her as my heart
    rate more than doubles

INTROSPECTION

The Park-N-Me

Heaven, help me remember how to get to you
I'm not exactly certain what I'm supposed to do

Don't recall the places that I have been
Or names or faces of my next of kin

They say I am sixty or thereabouts
Can no longer hold a pencil, shaky bouts

When I speak to the people around me
They finish the sentences of my stories

Often I fall asleep in places that I sit
I would eat more often, but I forget

Sometimes I get lost when I walk the halls
Surely I am not partial to the smell or bright white walls

I am almost sure my name is Burt or Stanley
Please let me know if you see my family

A Letter To Anyone Who Might Care

Dear Sir or Madam,

The reason for this correspondence you will soon be able to tell

Writing means so much more than its words suggest on the page when reaching out from jail. For today, I don't have freedom. If my words make it out of here, each one releases a bit of my soul from hell. So often I have written someone, reaching out for compassion from a family member or a friend, to no avail. Every day at 6 AM when my name is not called at mail call, it makes me want to yell. I am writing anyone this Dear John letter because it seems I have become life's unknown stranger, and it's just as well.

Thank you, kind sir or madam. Your acceptance of this letter has allowed my emotional upheaval to quell

P.S.   There really is no need to write back from freedom's stomping grounds where I once was but from which I fell

Sincerely,

L.D.

Lies

My guard it surely fell
I saw heaven's earthly angel

A vision's quizzical gaze
Caught in a dream's maze

Truly beauty's prodigy
No less a goddess breed

My knees got so weak
Voice heard soft and sweet

Heart, it just gave out
Emotions strewn about

Love's keeper is fate
Words you illustrate

You're my incessant desire
Smoldering soul's ember fire

As each day begins
Simply just won't end

Known, there is no feeling
Fills rooms floor to ceiling

Woman of my dreams
A man without his Queen

Dark are the nights
Love remains from sight

Forever I'll keep trying
Without you I am dying

Togetherness that has died
Maybe my dreams have lied

Untitled

Funny thing about my poems, read once again
They strike me as if I never wrote one. Is that a sin?

Not sure how or why this is, read once again
Each seems as new as a gift at Christmas. Is that a sin?

Probably has little to do with age, read once again
Or volume, page after page after page. Is that a sin?

Condescending to say words come easily, read once again
No one poem has truly pleased me. Is that a sin?

Often it seems I'm bragging, read once again
Listen to a grown man's nagging. Is that a sin?

What do my poems do for people, read once again?
Provide a key for their keyhole? Is that a sin?

Give them insight, words of love, read once again?
Display my battles, push and shove. Is that a sin?

Hints to what's in my soul, read once again
A brain, a mind that has more pull. Is that a sin?

Many I've written dark, wrath of Hell, read once again
Free or not living life imitates jail. Is that a sin?

Questioned or located sense of divinity, read once again
Coming or going of who I am supposed to be. Is that a sin?

One thought's end allows another to begin, read once again
I will continue filling pages with this poet's pen. Is that a sin?

Senses

The sight of moonlit wave tops, thundering and crashing onto a rocky beach

Smells of a breeze-free, dew-heavy orchard with one giant fur-fuzzed peach

To hear Sunday's sacrament from the Vatican, my soul's evil it would leech

Again to hold my children as infants, an emotion greater than any word of human speech

Lord, if I'm resurrected, these are my sense's wishes. Please keep them within my reach

Poetry

Should I write long lines or write short lines?
How should I start the poem's beginning, or choose words for its end?
Should I or shouldn't I make my words rhyme this time?
These are a few of the challenges I face, poetry's hows, whats, and whens

Words fall into harmonic verse, perfectly chosen for form
Do poet's words' understanding get lost within works that chime?
Or do they seem to stumble and stammer when broken from the norm?
Misconveyed conceptions, wandering, lost out of time

Poets throughout the ages and their works are often smitten
Frost, Mueller, Emily Dickinson, and Edgar Allan Poe
They captivated the world over who read them or have listened
Each formulated genius incomprehensible, yet I long to know

I also want my works to be great, admired, cherished through time
When I am gone, I want my words to remain for all readers to adorn
I want them to know I wrote feverishly, a madman out of his mind
Leave a bit of a legacy like my four heroes in poetry, as if heaven born

Poetic work the hows, the whats, and the whens
Fruits of a labor of love, hard work, rarely feed one only the rind
My poems from beginning to end, long lines, short lines, or words
    that may or may not rhyme
I assure you all this I love to write and the poem's words will always
    be mine

Will

Hunkered down inside I am, unable to guess time's hour
Darkness serves a cold, bitter taste of fear and bile sour

Devilish game where rules are not written, demonic souls induction
The right for life bankrupt, moral failure leads to dysfunction

Shadowy evil's location unknown, though ever present in the room
Smells of tear's trails of salt and fear that loom

Imagined is a safe, warm place far away from here
Far away from a wet, stained bed, from bleeding wounds and tears

Reaching out to God with white knuckles and clenched fists
Begging for mercy and for my life not to end like this

My Lord, is there no heavenly angel from the suffering I have found?
At once, I am lifted from the bed, thrown on the stone cold ground

"No way out! Oh, my Lord in heaven, help me, hear me please
As I crawl across what seems like broken glass on my hands and knees"

Delirious at this point, consciousness now drifts in and out
Thoughts of no greater pain imaginable, control is strewn about

Between life and death, no rest in this sick and twisted kingdom
Where hell's orders are freely given and reaper's deeds are done

Sounds inaudible, closing in from afar
Cannot tell from where or tell exactly what they are

At this moment, I wonder if the sound is from heaven's gate
Listening, laying still in the dark abyss, impossible to negotiate

Thereafter, I recognize a scent of summer's rain
Ensuing the wonderful scent, the ripping of my flesh. I scream in pain

Surely each and every breath is short, such is life and time
Something is about to give, my soul, my body, or my mind

Shivering and quaking in fear and pain, I tumble side to side
Death, take me now in your carriage, end this horrific ride

At once my eyes adjust to the moon's beaming light
Realizing that in my dream, I had lost my will to fight!

Mortals Need Heroes

Alone in my room, eclectic thoughts share my space

The noise is harmonically deafening, concentration is silenced

Beautiful trees outside blow, wind hurts us

Empty, food reminds me now of places and people

Can I be loved enough by both?

Fences, pants rolled up, fulcrum is my crotch

Desire, I am grateful to your thoughts and memory

Life is dumbfounding but I can't really tell, oddly

My loss for words is not from being speechless

Life, bite after bite, "Manners, please!"

Don't talk to strangers with your mouth full, glass half

My Pops is very much alive. You do not compare

Angelic auras glow bright, his is the sun, professed greatness, mine

Train into a collegiate station, all enter, enlightened, composed is he

We mortals need heroes and teachers, and hope he understands

As Candlelight Wanes

Behind me, ironically, she calls my name
How could this be, so soon? My mind shuddered and labored
Not yet a week has passed since our bodies were one in the same
Love took to flight, like Icarus filling the sky as a bird

Tone in her voice began my projection of hope in unwinding
Right then, hinting to me, love we would not bolster
Foiled once again, reasons my ears need not reminding
Soul mate's love may never be at my side as a gun in a holster

Turning toward the voice nervously, but remaining close to calm
Although my swollen heart was trying to escape from my chest
Blasé, I said "Jennifer, I didn't see you, what's going on?"
As if God's most beautiful angel blends in with heaven's rest

"Been working lots of hours, and these kids, ugh!" she said
Brightness in her eyes very different than at candlelight's wane
Confounded, was it Jennifer whose heart I so misread?
Had I scratched my name or her soul and bedpost, leaving there a
    stain?

A lump in my throat ensued; I could not talk or swallow
Such a twist of fate, Lord how could this be?
Thought of her pain, she in need, left me empty and hollow
Taken aback by circumstance, all I could say was "Just hug me"

30

For 30 years, I have been at war with myself. Can't you tell?
All the while poised for my obituary for death, mind and body in
   living hell

At this point, I cannot stop what long ago I had begun
I have always viewed my end, the release of my soul, with drugs
   and a gun

Troubling thing is that all this time, I never convinced myself to
   stop
Partially due to being alone in life and in loneliness, what benefit
   is there to cop?

I am sure that in no time, I will deliver my last and final blow
When I do, I plan on doing it quietly so that no one will ever
   know

My life's ways were never close to being pure as driven rain
I pray every day there is no resurrection because that would mean
   I would have to live and die again

Trapped by my way of thinking, it has always been me I hate
Now I see no reason to live, no clear pathway to negotiate

Every breath, every moment, death's rush is a crush I am having
To put an end to the punches jabbing

Guess I have always been just a bit too weak to make it through
God, it just turned 30 years now that I have truly needed you

Love In The First

Your glamour, your beauty
Elegance, charisma to the nines
So well-versed, yet unrehearsed
Left a victim's curse
Could you be mine?

Se well-rounded
Totally grounded
My heart's pounded
Love in the first

Woman to fruition
Not to mention
Comprehension

Loves to listen
Aura glistens
Lord's gifted blessing
You I am missing

Well?

So I have been told, I wish you well. And for me, that statement brings to mind an interesting question

Is it in some way or is it in every way your way of lowering me down into life's quickly forgotten chamber of darkness and its bottomless abyss?

Or is it your way of tossing another coined phrase at me while your foot is on my head as I'm drowning, hoping life will applaud your lack of empathy and grant you one wish?

If that's the case, what would you wish for as my body, my soul, slowly disappears into the murky bowels of the black, life-stripping water?

Would you ask for forgiveness from your God or your spiritual higher power for what you have done and thought?

Would you hope to be given a line and the strength to rescue me from impending doom, an act so unselfish in thought?

Or would you further my descent until I vanish, hoping all the while the well grants you your wish, giving you the most for your coin and what it had bought

Vows, My Way

It's not a fair battle, our very last chord
A knife at a gunfight before the Lord

Vows were so strained it was like doing time
Neither knowing when ours became yours and mine

Our frantic appeals each could never hear
Children at our sides, living in fear

The fuse was lit with no way to circumvent
The damage we had done each other irrelevant

We said we won't listen and we can't ever mend
No time for each other until the end

A retrospective of us is never that easy
But I figured it out - it was me out to please me

Now I want you to know that seven years later
I have found my true love and I'm no longer a hater

Very Young

From very young, I tried to follow the rules
Did things unadmired, set a home on fire, went from school to
    school

From very young, I tried to follow the rules
I needed all the attention, got locked away in detention, but I was
    sure nobody's fool

From very young, I tried to follow the rules
I was usually the smallest, but I sure fought like the tallest and I
    thought I was cool

From very young, I tried to follow the rules
I probably would never have made it unless my Mom was the greatest

In retrospect, I've sure been a fool.

Two-Leaf Clover

Got me one hell of a losing streak
There is no aspect of living I am able to beat

This kind of thing is getting to me and bringing me down
I'm the world's unluckiest person around

Easy to see that life is trying to put me on my ass
If this is one of God's big tests, I sure hope I pass

I realize living is not supposed to be one big peach
But just once, I'd like to kick off my shoes and play at the beach

I'm not asking a lot, like asking to rule the free world as its
    president
But if ever I had big goals and dreams, they just came and went

So I am living here in America, land of opportunity and freedom
But my luck has drained from my horseshoe, leaving me a two-
    leafed clover kingdom

Twisted Dreams

What will I become, who will I soon be
When I leave the walls of this facility?

Will I learn and grow, or will I run aground?
Will I slip away without a single sound?

Will I pass the tests, allowing my past to guide my way?
Will the words "I'm sorry" follow my failures again, day after day?

A life so twisted, it's as if time stopped and shattered
Chances given were sacrificed by selfishness, as if I was all that
    mattered

I'm not a man unworthy of happiness or dragged down by the stone
I'm not this screwed up person who wants to be alone

So with the task at hand, can I make my family proud?
'Cause I'm tired of crying in my dreams with silent screams so loud

Upstream

I wonder why you were the only one who never ran
When the great floods came after the steady rains began

All the while, you were the only one who stuck it out
Guess you believed in me and what I was all about

To this day, there has never been a reason for me to believe in me
Truth known, in the mirror I've never liked who or what I see

God, I am surprised that I have made it this long
Without life's tune playing my funeral song

Life has been rough for me since I was a child
Not even I could come close to contain me, so wild

No doctor, not pills, or even another's suggested love
Could curb my ways when push came to shove

At this point, I've cried enough to flood all the world's avenues
And I'm tired of swimming upstream, just like you

Under Me

Now she is out from under me
Said she needed time to breathe

On the altar we were blessed
She never looked back, I was dismissed

So many things I still want to say
12 years now, unable to find my way

All my hurt hidden behind my smile
Maybe today's the day she'll call, it's been a while

I'm trying to move beyond the pain I mask
One more chance is all I ask

The past isn't over. Can't we try again tomorrow?
Leave behind all our trivial history swamped in sorrow?

Cast away all our positions we said we would not compromise
Wish I could look one more time into your eyes

Touch your face and run my fingers through your hair
I'm so lost without you; I thought we would always be a pair

Turn Around!!

It starts with a phone call then your carriage awaits
Fearful and broken inside, a past of bad traits

Between the clamor of doors and starless filled nights
Eerie cries for forgiveness with nothing to fight

As we walk down the hallway before a God of our own
Sweat seethes from our bodies to reap the seeds we've sown

A fruit none shall harvest but those in nice ties
The poor and ill soon forgotten to the system's demise

The Hunt

Once upon a time, I felt I was a part of humanity
Then I tired of gobbling up miles of crap from those who projected
    vanity
Now solitude through psychosis, it leaves the adrenalin in me
    staged with insanity

Brandishing delicious ill will, inflicting pain and fear into those
    with the sound of my voice
From under my psychotic rock, I am coiled, ready, in attack
    position so poised
Rattled, hear me now and fear me later, in time you won't have a choice

Being held hostage, this decision of yours must truly be daunting
This game I play is my safari ride, cleaning my weapon, ready for
    the hunting
Soon after you decide, you will realize that I was the one in
    control throughout and it was your life I was taunting

13

—∘∘∘❉◈❉∘∘∘—

I use loneliness as my flashlight to slip deeper into each moment
and upcoming night's darkest of secret woods

With the changing of my towns and the states of my heart that
land upon a like soul more often than the changing of my
bed sheets

13 years cast aside, I am no longer a part of the presence of honor
brought on by the grip of once interlocked fingers

An evolution through retrospect, a metamorphosis of an undying
love, ready for its granite marker, with time tilling it further
into dirt

Man's Ruin

Industrial disease
Blowhole to heaven
Mother Earth Bleeds
Continents seven

Carbon emissions
Glaciers melting
No humanity submission
Actions not helping

Scientific dumb down
Tainted water
Forests disappearing around
Acid rain aquifers

Hazardous pesticides
World befools
Chemical suicide
No renewable fuels

Wars lashing ages
Political caroling
Biblical gauges
Treaties dishonoring

Responsibilities vilified
Futures to rethink
Reaper stands by
Species extinct

The Anthem of Risk

Poised for my attack from across the sea of green
With bullets in hand now, my intentions are mean
A slighted feeling of chance that time may redeem

Sitting around all, not knowing what I'm holding
I give the three a glare, the situation ever molding
Doubling the stakes, there's no chance of my folding

Remembering the past and that it's an eye for an eye
One, two, three, they fall down from the sky
Two women are showing and some guy with one eye

Two of three standing, I randomly check
Emotions uneasy, flopping around, I'm a wreck
My gun still has bullets so I say "what the heck"

Too deep in the game to lie down and quit
The turn falls from the heavens, one I'd like to forget
Executing another bad gamble my hand now unfit

Pinned down by bullets, I jump into the river
My mouth is so dry the angst makes me shiver
I get one more bullet, more ammo for my quiver
Aces full over Queens, now pass me the silver!

I

—∘∘∘❦◈❦∘∘∘—

I want to know if I have lived like I am dying, don't we all?

I want to win, not just recover a little

I want to know that if I am everyone's friend, who and where are they?

I want to know the world's greatest Dad. Wouldn't that be God?

I want to know if it is better to care a lot or to be pissed very seldom

I want to know that if your kids are the most beautiful and the smartest, are everyone else's ugly and dumb?

I want to meet a timely death

I want to be a part of something less great than me

I want to be on the wrong side of the unlawful

I want to wake on the right side of the bed

I want to know I'm in love without falling

I want to be good but not as good as the people I surround myself with

I want to cut into the front of the long line of great writers

I want to find out what will make my kids' kids grand

I want to know before all good things that must come to an end what they are, so I can plan. I hate surprises

I want to know, because I have heard we only meet our soul mates twice in our lives, would it help if I wore a name tag?

I want to know where a kleptomaniac keeps everything, including each of his grains of salt

The Corporate Elevator

It is great, this life, when lived inside a bubble
A vacuum of perception while breaking unwritten rules

A packed tea party in an etiquetteless elevator, exchanging wildly
staring gazes
Plastic smiles served up quickly on a porcelain, gold-rimmed
saucer of anxiety

And the denials of trouble permeating senses
Most notable that of fear's silence

Fear from desperation and the unnerving pressure of perpetual
deadlines unmet
Fragrant in another's inability to gain control of a wonderful-
smelling lack of morality

Errr!

This aimless soul through which in life I wander

The essence of time is nothing meant that I freely squander

A trove of "what could have beens" rarely do I ponder

The list so great, my soul would ache as if a hypochonder

Asked "What if?", a difficult question as prospective responder

I have lived as I have wanted. I could not contentedly be fonder

To responsibility and freedom, I am the great absconder

Thirst

To transcend time, my poems can't, but you do

Your long fingers, hands of time, clock stopping father's hands, German

My hands short, perfect feet, mother's no doubt

Hope, thirsty in your eyes, angelic 6, a water blue

Mine dark, so hers

Humor over, a lonely life, my empty home

Her smile, daddy's rile, abstain, ex again

I can't forgive me. Would you, could you, don't you?

Understand?

You know, I want to walk and talk like all the famous folks
Out for a stroll, I want to remind them of my greatest quotes

It is high time Crayola names a new color after me
Make me feel almost godlike, like the guy who parted the sea

I want to be like that Alex on Jeopardy, all-knowing
When time comes to compare scars, I want my awesome one showing

I need to prove to anyone that I am the world's greatest dad
Follow that up by letting them know they are the best friend I've
    ever had

Give me control and I will show you a conversation language of
    nothing but cusses
When I go downtown, I want to show off my picture on the side
    of buses

Really, I want to go out to dinner and talk about books that I've written
Be the center of attention, hey that's me, got a moment to listen?

I think I need to hire one or two full-time personal assistants
Have them do all my shopping for me, even pick out their own presents

I will drive around in my free time in the most bad-ass cars
Get thrown out of a night club, just to brag and say that it's my bar

Step on the heads of the critics who chastised me and my books
Never look back while laughing at name badge wearing crooks

I will be the guy you give a dollar to and watch it turn into a dime
I will treat you as well as you did me, if I can find the time

Much is for certain in this crazy world that we live in
One thing is, it's a much better ride in the driver's seat, so come
    on, get in

Now the clouds seem to part for me, almost in rapture
As dreams out of reach a year ago already I've captured

So much has happened since I put this pen into my right hand
If I don't recognize you or answer your calls, just try to understand

Sandpiper

Never is the shape of a cloud unfamiliar

Insanity, failure, the tastes readily forgotten

Ever are green and determined, trampled grasses still growing

Does guilt ever put me beside myself?

Lost at sea, are birds around to guide me?

Prayers made in waters deep are rarely answered

I want to hear the white noise of the ocean breeze

Tempt fate, like a sandpiper on a rainy beach

Contentedly chirping a song, full, guiltless, collecting food, grasses

Answers given by a rainbow chasing waves, life full

Need You

Look at me with my hair gelled back
My stylish two-hundred dollar shoes
Designer jeans and my silken shirt, tailored to fit
Now all I need is you

Listen to me, with my fifty-cent words
To make you believe I'm the Who's Who
A voice so strong, swooning you like a poet
Now all I need is you

Pray for me. With latter years upon me now, I never found my
    one, that's true
I've looked and sounded the part
Bury me and pray for me, with my broken wallet and broken heart
Now all I need is you

Tears

What are the reasons and the things that make us cry?
For some, it's brought on by an emotional letdown or a fib or a lie
For others, it has to be hugely tragic, like when someone close to
them dies

I've witnessed many times before, crying for a depressive change in
the season
Then there are those who don't really know why
They cry for no apparent reason

A child's first day of school brings tears flowing
Especially when the bus pulls away
That's when the flowing gets double going

Some will cry when thinking back into their past
Many will cry to let go of the pressure that's built up
A way to make an ugly feeling not last

Grown men cry when their favorite team has won a challenge, and
event, or a game
Parents will cry when they hold their beautiful babies for the first
time and call them by name

I have watched people cry because of a current and epic drama like
a news event
Sometimes people cry for so long, it's as if the tears will never relent

Whether it is tears of happiness or tears of joy, that is for your own
mind to sort
But may the next tears that fall down your face bring your soul
and life great comfort

Swing

—∘∘○❈○∘∘—

I wonder who and what I will be today?

The one who is called by some a mindful father,
or the one who says please, do not bother?

The one you would proudly call your son,
or the one who is self-centered, always his number one?

The one who stands for and says everything cool,
or the leader of no one beyond just a fool?

The one that you love from the moment he arrives,
or the no-call and no-show with red, bloodshot eyes?

The one who is strong with the world's weight on his back,
or the one who's positioned himself for an attack?

The one who makes love well into each night,
or the one that you know when something's not right?

The one you can count on, a truly great friend,
or the one praying "God, will this crap ever end"?

The one who is grateful when our relationship advances,
or the one who is evil, giving emotionless glances?

I guess that I'll try just to be me for a day,
or until my next mood swing sweeps me away

Suffering

I woke up one morning and I picked up the page
Financial crisis, its woes were all the rage
Asked myself what could I do to help that today
So I got my pen and checkbook and gave it all away

Woke up broke the next day, picked up the page
Viral disease was all the rage
Asked myself what could I do to help today
So I went to the doctor and gave a kidney away

Woke up the next day broke and with only one kidney, picked up
the page
More terrible suffering in the world all the rage
Asked myself what could I do to help today
Went back to the doctor and told him to donate all my organs and
my soul, give them away

Doctor looked at me and smiled, and then he said "OK"
For the doctor realized I could not live without my organs and
soul, and I would no longer have to suffer, as he took all my
pain away

51 Or Thereabouts

Amidst radio waves and the now active dirt trails leading in and
away from the ghost towns of 51
Where thermometers had reached, and history's almanac recorded,
heat hot as the surface of a blazing sun

Harnessed lightning desire as the king's men danced around
the sprawling campfire, witnessed with champagne and
fashionable glasses
Torrents of oddities occurred since the heavens umbrella hellish-
size cloud, stop, drop, tuck. Rods are falling on classes

Gunslinger-type bar fights, the Wild West kind, where, if you lost,
someone bought you a drink. 100,000 lives weren't dead
Science's rat race quickly changed those rivalries with a flash, still
fought at ground zero from hospital beds

Fission and fusion ushered out the industrial age and the cowboy
outlaw, deciding the good guy and who has the powers
Recourse being, now even planes are to be considered weapons of
mass destruction after flown into great towers

For good or bad and for rich or poor, I wish I had a time machine
to go back and live in days vanished one hundred or more
years
Away from these modern, crazy days of terrors, projection of fear,
and utter chaos of religious lunacy
Put a six-shooter at my side and protect my family and my
homeland the way it was meant to be

Back to a much simpler era when banks and nations did not need
some great American government bailout
A simpler day and time it was then, long before our desert storms
and the area of number 51's massive fallout

Scholar?

Often I sit and wonder what it would be like to be a scholar
Would my words that I write make women swoon and yell to me
"Holla"?

Would my words be analyzed to the nth degree like the words in
the bible are?
Could they get me nice things when I write them, like a party
boat or a race car?

Maybe if I chose all the right words to write, I would never need
to speak
Let them do all the talking for me, making me provocative,
mysterious, and some kind of freak

Could my words have amended the constitution or saved our
soldiers from battle?
I guess with the way this country sets precedents and creates law,
would that even matter?

Would my words have been archived for future generations to take
another look?
Or should they have stayed in my mind forever, because the time
you gave to read them was something I took?

Stars

Lying awake, waiting for the stars to run
Chased away by the rising sun

For it is in the night
My fears take off in flight

Comfort difficult to attain as one
Waiting for the stars to run
Chased away by the rising sun

I place my head in my hands
Think hard and try to understand

How long ago this disease had begun
Waiting for the stars to run
Chased away by the rising sun

Six feet now in the ground
No sunlight or sound
No one ever around

My mortal life done
Chased away by the stars, lit by the sun

Absentee

Three willows in the wind, together I do adorn
Alone, the face of evil is no less than scorn

Photographs take their places in one's memory
A visual in a home on a mantle where thoughts should be

Collecting dust their borders, the shelf, sands of time
Projections of torture, the forgotten, yours, not mine

November brings hope my memory will be updated
With no holiday frames that read "Rest in Peace"
For one year's time I should feel elated

Flooding Déjà Vu

The clockworks hands have extended to me a date for great
retrospect and a motion to levy an unsatisfied conviction

Moments collected by larger blocks of times; hours day months
and years, weathered the salty machine of time, its face long
and droll

Cast upon the stage, curtain call for mercy and repentance at the
black-robed dress, his feet, me the length of time's coming
attraction

Time is abound with its body being always round, grotesque –
unpleasant to all who look at it as is when elite passing above
glimpse, a bridge guarding troll

Surreal is this day, yet how best to convey complications of
mysterious wonders by a trove of coincidence that channel a
feeling of flooding déjà vu

Just as would a comedy of erroneous acts follow in sweet
repetition, giving me something to ponder and laugh at, as
odd as when each time I put on new socks, the same toe
escapes to tickle my shoe

Then one pair, two pair, ten pairs more with each time I go back
to my dresser, it seems like the socks I throw away somehow,
just as quickly as I could return to my drawer, make it back

Moving ironically onward or so it would so dreadfully seem, in
choosing the last pair there in which my neck had craned

This told, all I needed to know as my surreal day to follow and the
gavel of Magistrate's conveyance and could the hands of time
pick me up, waking me from my less than celestial slumber's
dream

Electricity bolted through my body, curled my toes, and its
lightning flash heat cut through my shoe and foot's harness,
my stocking, the hole, it had fixed it

Along my day, throughout my way, I trotted aware without
concern, mindful I've nothing in and of this day to fear, short
of his pounding gavel of swift despair

160

When that falls down, I will proudly show it to everyone around
as if it were the most brilliant jewel upon his crown, my head
severed atop his white fence's picket

Laughing along my day, hands of time not getting in my way,
each pointing me in directions of circles for which I show no
concern for its guidance to follow desires yearned

Dreaming of the wrath of the magistrate and the events that may
transpire regarding some non-eventual fictitious date, a healed
mind or soul, never will they correlate to perpetuate to seal my
fate

Life has given us all retrospect, a far more relevant tool to gauge
blame. Compare it to the hands of evil or good, clockworks
barometer, watch it and in no time astound at what you have
quickly learned

A sentence, a dream, an emotion surreal or ironic, is nothing lest
we mix them with time, thought, and with genuine heartfelt
concern

Our Martyrs

Doing battles
Cannot retreat
Cannot sleep
Gotta' stay on our feet

Collateral damage
Wide and abroad
Felt in opera boxes
And Broadway stars

Planes into buildings
Bombs inside cars
Chasing bad guys
When the martyr's ours

From nation to nation
Redeeming our blood
Dropping our bombs
Killing more of our young

Ten years later
Trillions out the door
None here any safer
Can she take much more?
America, can we please truly end our wars?

Seasons

Seasons
    Another passes on by
    More steam shown on my cup of coffee
Now
    Winter approaching quickly, the reason

Seasons
    My heart swells with great sadness
Now
    Gone is warmth, the sun's rays

Seasons
    Left naked and empty
Now
    Just as are all of the trees

Seasons
    Ushered in the halting of growth
Now
    Winter ending, fall on life's knees

Seasons
    Ruggedly, so not friendly
Now
    Warranted signal to young and old

Seasons
    One to follow the other
Now
    After the cold

Devices

Wish there were devices made to cover up my past
Something to quell the guilt and shame I have amassed

History's reality cloak made just for me and perfectly tailored
So I can accept all of my imperfections and faults, I pray my Lord

For me to hide myself from myself and from what others may find
From a disastrous, hurtful history that continues to creep up from
    behind

Moving me stealth-like into my and others eyes of love, respect,
    and grace
So I no longer hate me, tuck my tail from others, and run in place

She's My America

Lord, bless our America, this country where all people can truly
   becomes what's in their dreams
Where majestic mountain ranges and forests were strategically
   placed by You, or so it seems

So fertile are her hills, valleys, and plains, she produces food for
   every continent in the world
Where a mighty river cuts a canyon so grand, simply from the
   force of its water's hurl

A nation that stands for and promotes freedom and democracy
   from country to country
She strives for, and is a testimony to, racial and gender civil liberty
   through constitutional equality

My Lord and America, I thank you for each day in which I am
   within your borders
The U.S.A. is my home, and for over 200 years, she has been
   kicking ass, not taking orders

Smile

There are so many different things in this world that make people
smile
Like the comfort of a hug and a kiss, followed by "I love you", or
"See you in a while"

You can make someone do it almost all of the time, no matter
their mood, when tickled, so wild
Others never put theirs away it seems, donning one from ear to
ear. You can spot them for miles

Many will never share theirs with you, but get them around a
number they will, as in money compiled
I have seen them occur in the strangest times and places, like in a
court of law after a verdict on trial

Then there are those of relaxed, happy comfort, like a long awaited
vacation or a trip down the Nile
I've witnessed many that were born of total frustration. Nervous
energy makes people do that when their insides get riled
See them often at sporting events or games for some
accomplishment, an award, a victory, or title

You know, sometimes I just laugh at myself and smile a whimsical
grin
Whatever makes you smile, may you do it over and over again.

Go Team, Go!

Retrospect is life's great parallax
History's events never change their facts
Once a moment passes, we can never bring it back

Events will happen out of one's grasp
As if snake-bitten by karma's asp
Goals and dreams get bumpy like a rasp

Planning ahead is never done in vain
Where nothing is ventured, there is no gain
Remember, sometimes sunny days will have some rain

Life throws obstacles at you and in your way
Quitters never win on their very best day
The game of life is won only when we continue to play

Dotage

The dotage of time
Less than kind
Feeble the mind
Whimpers, whines

'Til all is lost
Washed away, forgot
Forget me not
Six-foot earth slot

Left all alone
Retirement homes
Family not shown
Confusion thus roams

One-hundred eighty degree chills
Shaky from pills
Changing of wills
Tears on windowsills

Spouse long since died
Lord, have you lied?
Well-being denied
Life's end lonely ride

My grave sighted
Destination plighted
Nothing is oversighted
Death's never recited

Vision, Blinded

Held captive by our actions and reactions and by our tongue's
    words that don't bear repeating
Chewing at the underbelly of what is and could be, both take an
    undeserved beating

Challenged by the "this time is mine" along with the blood-letting
    of our past, colored black and blue
We dangle our hearts on a string, positioning one another, a
    puppet pointing and saying "right back at you"

Progressive in nature are both the good and the bad, one another
    setting ablaze under the fabric of our being
Blinded by situational sensations and learned behavior with
    disregard of positive visions to come and what the other is
    seeing

Solstice

Hearts and branches are weighted so heavily
Storm's night snow fell fierce and steadily

Crystalline diamonds caught by morning light
Goose-down flakes stacked on alike

God's breath's gentle breeze the only sound
A courageous witnessing bunny the only emotion around

New day's blinding sun glares off the horizon
Vision of change for those that dare lay eyes on

Sun's warming rays signal one thing
Winter's season beauty ushers in spring

Dream's Groom

A curtain of fear fell over her face, a pale veil of impending doom
Pushed up from the carpet-like sea of green grasses, arose like fate
from a wedding cake's groom

Her tonic was staunch that stormy summer's day. Scared, she
shivered with chills
Hurriedly, in one desperate moment and motion after what she
saw, she tried to knock reality back with handfuls of pills

"You can't be real!" she screeched aloud, "So go away at once. Just
leave me the hell alone!"
"Get out of my mind, I command you. Back to your dirt nap.
Climb into your box in your earthen grave's home"

It was at that exact moment she was taken aback by the icy cold terror
Her face so contorted with surprise and fear, she would not
recognize herself in a mirror

Veins bulged from her temples, gulping for air as if drowning in
unforgiving waves of a blood-thick ocean
Choking with the succession of each wave greater than the last,
forcibly filling her lungs with the devilish potion

"God as my witness", she prayed, "I beg of you my Lord for all
your tender mercy upon my life's soul that you could possibly
give!"
"I shall follow your commandments, Lord. I will repent of all my
transgression. I will walk in your name if you allow me to live

Suddenly, a surreal calm came over her quavering body and her
quaking soul came to rest. Yet in looking around, no evidence
of a miracle's feat
Then upon rising to stand, she collapsed back into the bed where
she had been seemingly sleeping, now trying to calm her
convulsing heart's beat

There she awoke the next morning in the same position in which
  she had fallen into deep sleep the remainder of the night
All seemed as it should, but what went on in that room could not
  be explained or forgotten, leaving her chest feeling tight

At 11:59 AM that very day, she walked arm in arm with her Father
  through the "Great Doors" that lead to an altar at the far end
  of the room
At the end of the aisle, she remembered her promise to God that
  she made in her dream and those in the latter, her vows, giving
  the bride her groom

Spring

Amidst all the refreshing springtime showers

The landscape is blooming triumphantly with flowers

Animals abound, some near, some far

Under the sun's warming rays

Otters under the canopy of night and stars

For many, it is their first taste of spring

Learning and seeing what it's all about

They frolic and play, do that type of thing

Running through lush forests and fields

Swimming in the creeks with the trout

For those who have been through springtime before

Great time to relax and stuff food in their mouths

Stars

Chasing stars through fractured windows
Letters of intent written, yet not ready to send those

There is a massive weight upon my emaciated chest
My mind so convoluted and tortured, it cannot rest

So heavy the gray area of my disease between black and white
Ever present, the disturbing feeling that nothing's ever right

Dangerous and terrific are my visions, to what expense no telling
Living beyond mortal fears without God, it's me you hear yelling

Lying on the table, the only thing I own is my soul, to waste
Disdain has again become my tongue's only taste

Destination unforgiving and unknown, knees soon buckle and
weaken
A father, a brother, a son, a friend, a soul, down the drain from
tweeking

Princely Guy

You are the only part of me I would never change
I think you are absolutely amazing, I beg of you to stay the same

I remember when we first met that autumn, in September
Inside and out, you are more beautiful now that I can ever remember

All these years later, and you are still the apple of my eye
You kissed a toad and you turned me into this princely guy

My shooting star is you, and I wish for us each day
If wishes and fairy tales could come true, you would love me
     forever, never going away

REFLECTIONS

King And Queen

Ring rays grace upward toward heaven above, day's end horizon
Splashing outward, an explosion amidst a now setting sun

Night coming, the queen seeks her dominance, climbing onto her
    throne
Ruling darkness, jewels revealed or not, setting the tone

Day drifts away, tucked into bed by sunset's sweet lullaby
Brilliance not shown, tomorrow's dawn brings another try

Rest now, life's king, for soon shall you be summoned to awake
Apocalyptic plague for granted forever's slumber should you take

Light years from present, your kin shown themselves as stars
Echoes caress the great nebula, jewels sparkle as do Venus and
    Mars

Queen kisses the universe with her infinite expanse, black, deep
    night
Sun king shows beauty, gives life to those basking in his light

A What Would, Can Could, If Life

What would have been a life in which a flower's permeating smell
   was so repugnant?
Would it be picked in gesture for its beauty and still given,
   without its promise to deliver a next generation through its
   chain of seed and chance of life?

Can could one truly be guided and lifted by deity and divinity of
   a spiritual godliness of their Lord if never once had they not
   held at embrace a hand of the devil?

If life had not its death and light not its darkness, would
   fascination be humdrum?

For we exist in our universe where we revolve on an axis of
   opposites that directly need one another to fuel our spectrum
   of prospective interests, right and wrong, good and bad

Hollywood Knife

A nip, a tuck, a lifted butt
An eye, a nose, hide it well so no one knows

A breast, a peck, a tummy tuck
Make me look young, I don't give a f%@!

Suck in my hips, fatten my lips, let me check my cash flow again
Really, I can look like a Kardashian

I'll be back, so don't trip
I want to look like Johnny Depp

Not exactly what I imagined at 24
Now I'm a woman who looks like Harrison Ford!

Hunger

Foodless from the thoughtful without action

Feeds the world nothing but our garbage and verbiage

Capitalistic starvation encompasses slogans of no good do-gooders

As they do not do as good doers have done with their actionless
actions

Furthering the gaps between bridges, creating greater impasse

Skyscraper- tall soap boxes and impressive margins built with
ocean-deep pools below them

Brimming with expendable greens of a presidential confetti

The Bench

Alive are the melodies of my youth, symphonies of wonder,
projected upon and impressed into my soul by a living icon,
my Mother

The Steinway played, each touch of her hand on me and on the
keys filled our home with love and my soul with song

Gone now is that piano, yet the magic remains, still brimming
from my bosom, the feeling of love, the sounds while sharing
that bench

Autumn Night's Daydream

In the cover of darkness, Mother Earth's safety blanket protects all
    creepy, crawly things once again, at last
Seldom is the celestial beaming glow of a sliver crescent moon
    visible between moisture-heavy billowy clouds that pass

Flowers roll up their sidewalks and close for business, no longer
    allowing their customers in
Their fragrant scents and amazing colors get taken back by them
    throughout the night upon their milky stems

A lightning flash upon the horizon's arch shimmers a silvery
    white–blue off the trap of a vacant spider's web
Close by, an ant clings atop a flagpole grass, swaying gently to and
    fro in nature's breath's flow and ebb

Droplets of dew jewel every horizontal surface, positioned as if
    waiting to catch a falling star
By morning, the plateau's surface will purge its bounty, requesting
    its drips to not fall too far

From an earthen hole rises a rodent's nose, skeptical to leave its
    home, twitching fearful whiskers that surround it
Up on a branch not too far away, an owl's head spins front to back,
    then flies down to confound it

This time of year, autumn's leaves clank in their trees with sounds
    unique, like that of clashing porcelain dishes
And life's cycle makes its mark and carries on in daytime or a
    forest dark, beautifully wonderful as one's daydream wishes

Pinholes

An attic type world brims with its keepsakes held away. For why?
So none may see

When a memory as the day's sun goes to night, is not the new
moon's face still bright?

Is the darkness of one's soul lurking there, away from what is
sunlit and out of reach?

Will it be there where a universe washes itself of man in less than
the seven days of creation?

Darkness life's fabric, a nebula brain controls from which our
master views our deeds through the pinholes stars eyes

While an orchestra of light-years flow in life's river of a constant
and certain world of change

Young and Old

A new morning's blue sky this poet's backdrop
Dew gathered on grass, cars, roofs, and warming blacktop

Across a meadow, somewhere a bird chirps and larks
Breath of God still, perhaps he's not breathing
Ants climbing trunks to partake of the warming sap the tree is
    seething

Familiar smells of flowers as a child I learned
Taken back to those younger days long ago, yearned

Deliberate steps I walk on, I take a well-known path
Knowing living beauty ends when it succumbs to the reaper's
    wrath

Locked Box And Hasp

There was much to gain but I chose to remain blissfully ignorant
Comfortable with the entitlement I sought within unquestioned
    spaces and knowledge's answers
Mentally keeping my distance

Pillars of wisdom I shunned, so varied, so strident, so poignant
I kept them out of arm's reach, well-recognized, yet pushed from
    my mind's grasp
Their fundamentals might have bled through and crept into my
    foundation
Cries of distracting interest were far beyond my care and my
    mind's locked box and hasp

Guise

What's in a name USA?
For now our tribes have no game due to the signing of the pale
  one reneging
After the many worthless words of the treaties
For example, the one that was signed full of false hope after the
  slaughter at Wounded Knee

As the white riot ran through the spiritually sacred native pristine land
  while supposedly giving a helping hand, the massacre ensued
By the outmatched fired upon by the bangs of their newcomer's
  muskets
Killing their kin at will, the old, the young
All the while pretending it was them while raping their women
  who could be trusted

For our records being self-serving of course
We call them pioneers and our great mavericks and settlers
In recognizing the reality with unbiased thought
It is certain we were nothing more than the world's greatest meddlers.

Bringing vast change
And not to mention the worst of all mankind's disease
As the new frontier killed by the thousands
Fed by the fire of greed

So now it seems our symbol of strength
We stole as our own national icon
The bald eagle carries less meaning, less gumption
For its true master Mother cries less her hope of saving her tribes
  and their greater understanding

And worship her throughout
Not just in an eleventh hour bid brought on by fear
As her tears fall from her face
Pouring acid from her eyes, now science surely has proven
Yet we are told all is well and normal in her cycle, an obvious guise!

God's Country

A gentle wisp of crisp morning air breathes across a placid lake
Barely a ripple upon the mirrored reflection of the glacier-capped
    mountains did it make

Sun steadily rising as its first rays of warmth kiss good morning to
    the water's top and its surrounding sacred land
Signaling to the fish within its shores that it is time to feast on all
    the insects that fell victim to the night and eat all they can

Smells of cedar, pines, junipers, and of an off and distant campfire,
    permeate the pristine forest air
Lions, moose, bear, deer, antelope, squirrels, chipmunks, elk,
    eagles, woodpeckers, blue jays, just to name a few of the
    amazing animals in God's country that you can find there

Good Things

Climbing trees, we would laugh and shout
In the leaves, we thrashed about

We took off with our friends, riding bikes
At other times, we went for hikes

Man, we tore it up across the land
Swam at the beach, played in the sand

Skipped some stones out on the lake
Watched scary movies 'til way too late

In the summer, we did some camping
Sometimes played so hard, had to get a nap in

We would wrestle and play fight to see who was the toughest
We dyed our hair and all swapped clothes to see who was the
    coolest

We never put too much work into our schoolin'
But when the time came, the girls mattered, and we put the work in

In looking back, man, the time went by way too fast
No one tells you as a kid that it's the best time your life will ever
    have and that good things never last

Expendable

As the remainder take their flights back to our homeland
Our fortunate soldiers are done spreading democracy, AK in hand

This country's finest, their tours done from halfway around this world
Of a ten-plus year dance done on an unpopular stage doing the
    Jump, Shake, and Hurl

Finished playing hide and seek with Bush's deck of cards
How expendable our young American women's and men's lives
    truly are

When airplanes fly into buildings in our own damn country
Doesn't mean we cripple other civilizations as remedy

Billions spent and vast regions left in complete upheaval
Given freely were the lives of innocents thrown at the face of evil

End Child Abuse

Every night after I close my eyes
Evils subside and my soul takes flight

Nothing can hurt me on my magic ride
It is then I am free and no one can find me

Prayers answered lift me off my bloody knees
My spirit soars through the heavens with ease

Playfully chasing tails of falling stars
Wishing on each I could trade the abusive parents mine are

Eagle Eye

I can leap into the air and fly with just a single burst of air without flapping my wings

I fly with incredible grace and I can see for miles, spotting fish in a lake or my prey by a stream

I am not bald, although my name would suggest so. In fact, I am covered in feathers from the top of my head to the tip of my tail, so maybe I was named for my naked legs, talons to torso

I am an American icon, a symbol of strength, individuality, wisdom, and great freedom. I am said to be the fiercest of all god's feathered creatures in the sky

I guess that is a distinction as well as an honor to behold and be proud of. Right back at you, America, as I wink to your strength and beauty and applaud you, with one eagle eye

Dreams And Streams

Whimsical dreams
Times forgotten
Clear-running streams
Toxic and rotten

Choices made
Goals that fade
No night or day
Hoping I'll go away

A leap I leapt
A keep I kept
A deep so in depth, so surface a purpose
A dream past dreamt

A look I lost
The key I tossed
A speck, a spot
A card that shown
A blip, a dot
I think I thought

Began to begin
Unravel the raveled
I know the unknown
Expansive is nothing
My how I've grown!

Divine

Sweet the taste
A beacon prevails

Moonlit image perfection
Vision a rose

Warm heart's content
Stemming from strength

Blossoming sinless
Petals so shimmer

A harvested gesture
With undeniable posture

Delicate by design
So beautifully divine

Death Saints Manifest

Wounded and creeping along the fringes of shadows cast by a
    starry, moonlit night
Elated by the presence of blood, pulsing, tremored projectiles, and
    veins coursing adrenaline-filled rage, not right

Proudly but lethargically behind sideways shuffling steps of a
    formidable mental stability, the unblessed blind
Life's necessary nectar exiting profusely, weakening the fight or
    flight instinct that should have come to mind

A laying down of the shield of will, followed contently with arms
    folding, crossing over warm rivers of a fractured circulation
Better judgment thrown against the sword of a spiritualess
    manifest, the Death Saint and his murderous minions
    calculation
Fittingly, unnervingly cast out beneath purgatory's divide to reap
    their once-living sins, harvest their tallied equation

Satanic smiles, a promise as beautiful as a death purveyed in God's
    sanctuary, the Garden of Eden
Hell's helper, through insanity, gracefully punches your ticket and
    laughs as you fall bleeding

A now helpless soul your eternal receipt, a voucher tethered to sin,
    to enter death's quadrant
Harpless descent, less angelic entities to guide your pathway down
    and no way to ease the blistering heat felt by Hell's newest
    migrant

Color

Fly on, you beautiful little butterfly, fly
Beyond the blades of grass so low and above trees grown high
Upon your wings as they flutter
Bringing such amazing color to the sky

A wonderous journey, your destination I do not know
Year after year I'm bewildered as I watch those like you set sail and
    soar
Avenging those who have lost their life, as you shall too
All who have come before

In wind, rain, and hail, and in all types of weather
You forge on, regardless
Numbering one or in the millions
Being light as a feather

Your journey I envy
Because I know it's one of the toughest around
I can even appreciate you in death
As you bring so much color to the ground

Bullied

All seemed to start, I recall, in second grade
Awkwardly indifferent to those around
The way I walked, my attire, things I said
Easily a target if there ever was one to be found

Started seemingly innocent kid stuff after some classes
Through time what started as one saw the numbers grow
'Til I could study no longer, knowing I had to soon defend myself
    from the masses
Day after day, I was helpless. There wasn't a thing I could do

It was in the middle of sixth grade that I was bullied for the last time
Embarrassed and furious for four straight years now, picked on
Ran away from them to my home and I grabbed a loaded Glock 9
Went back to school, got my revenge, and left five dead on the lawn

America, stop the bullies!"

Boogie Men

Light unable to breach the night's abysmal fog
No telling from what direction come the wails of an agitated dog

Soon after bedtime, all complacent children are supposed to be asleep
It is out from under their beds and out from their closets we creep

Adults are unable to spot us with their pessimistic eyes
Upon their unrest, fearful children so gripped in terror, voiceless,
    are the wise

Eyes well up, still their emotions too afraid to even shed a tear
They pull their blankets over their heads to hide the fear

No music is heard or played as we dance to our boogie song
Ask a child. We boogie men have been real all along

Boo!

Black Widow

A tawdry web indeed is woven
Her prey set for those whose potential freedom is showing
Many a male succumb to her trap, unknowing

Pleasured by her, the temptress is presented so beautiful
All is in order as she sets a meal for one, pitiful

Dressed black as the night, the seductress dawns just a tease of red
Lures you into her home, then into her bed

Make love through the night, then you fail to awake at light's dawn
Another victim of fate by the Black Widow, your head is long gone

Big Town

I miss all the feel of a big town where my life's choices don't drum up a frown

A place that still holds a promise of hope for everyone in it and around

Where hard luck often ends at a rainbow's pot of gold and treasure found

An existence that on Sundays if you're not in their church, you're not put down

I can blend into the masses and not stick out like some circus clown

For once get through a first date without it ending on the topic of the price of a wedding gown

The big town's where my gaffs don't legally release on me a pack of gun-toting hounds

Where I am not the judge's example of the biggest criminal around

Autumn's End

All the trees' leaves are falling to the ground
With the signs of autumn's end, witnessed by all around

Withered, fruitless vines display the time for this reason
Life prepares itself for its upcoming winter season

Most fowl at this point have headed down South
Rodents prepared by storing their meals in a stockpile, mouth
    after mouth

For many animals, a journey began long prior, a winter's migrate
The bears forage all they can before their long winter's hibernate

The few who stay to stick it out get winter plumage or coats
Lucky are those who make it to spring, for winter's freeze is no joke

Angelic 7 (The Huntsman Tragedy)

Utah's wildly whispered screams not heard
A mother fired so many shots and the many who just turned

Almost three years gone before the find
Six were born and still alive, one had been the lucky, still,
    although I am sure the little angel tried

She felt she had to cover them up, man in prison, so she felt the
    need to hide them all, we say now
So I ask you, Utah, is it time to change your law?

To those who failed to give a damn
The blood is equally yours and on your hands!

For when we turn our backs on our ill
Often they will prove to us a hell beyond a cell and kill!!

But when the spiritually different or mentally challenged, the sick
    or for whatever reason those who in this state are not "just like
    them"
The burden gets too heavy to tote around your every sin!

Seven angels rest in peace now, Utah
Yet for ten years no one helped or talked to her

Where were all the cameras and the professionals then?
Where were the members of her family, the church, the news
    reporters or the daddies of the 7? Where were the sheriff's men?

Angels trapped under a broken wing, but the phone for help never rang.
All of those who watched the Huntsman tragedy unfold and did
    nothing for her or her Angelic 7 are just as guilty of the same sin

R.I.P., Angelic 7, R.I.P

America's Factory

Same ol' job, same ol' thing. Another day at the factory
Is this all I will ever become? Is this what life is cracked up to be?

Have I let this small town determine my destiny, my fate?
Doing a job a trained monkey can do while receiving half his rate?

Since this factory was built, it is all this little town has known
Now starved for its workers inside, no way out or hope is ever shown

Look around these factories. There are no college campuses or
    higher education
They pluck you right out of high school to fill orders and obligations

Fifteen years pass you by, and at thirty-three, you get laid off as a rule
Body so torn up from repetition, you can no longer use their tools